Menno-Nightcaps

MENNO-
NIGHTCAPS

Cocktails Inspired by that Odd Ethno-Religious Group
You Keep Mistaking for the Amish,
Quakers or Mormons

S. L. Klassen

TOUCHWOOD

This book is dedicated to all my friends on Mennonite Twitter and the loyal readers of the Drunken Menno Blog.

"[We] spent our time daily in playing, drinking, and all manner of frivolous diversions."

—Menno Simons*

*The Complete Works of Menno Simon, vol. 1, trans. John F. Funk (Elkhart, IN: John F. Funk, 1871), mennosimons.net/completewritings.html. Quote taken grossly out of context.

CONTENTS

Introduction 2

INTRODUCTION

I imagine you, dear reader, coming upon this little book and sizing it up from its title and cover.

I expect that you will have spied this book on a shelf or website and puzzled at its oddity.

You may have asked yourself, "What kind of joke is this?" To which I answer, "It is the best kind of joke, curious reader—the kind that comes with cocktail recipes."

I do not know if you came upon the book while looking for information about Mennonites or while looking for a cocktail book. In either case, you have lucked upon a long-overdue amalgamation of the cocktail book genre with whatever genre of books includes everything you never knew you wanted to know about Mennonites.

Here, you will find amusing commentary on Mennonite history, faith practices, and cultural forms, each with thematically appropriate cocktail recipes. While many books about Mennonites portray us as a simple people and many books about cocktails contain complicated recipes, I have reversed this pattern—highlighting the Mennonite complexities and offering up relatively simple cocktails.

Just because.

You may be thinking that you do not care about Mennonites. Or about cocktails. You might think we are boring, earnest types who wear old-fashioned clothes and sing a lot of hymns. You might think cocktails are fussy and complicated to make.

If you are thinking that, then you wouldn't be all wrong but you wouldn't be all right either. It is true that most Mennonites are boring and earnest, but we do not all dress in distinctive garb, and some of us will refrain from hymn singing in public. It is also true that some cocktails require precision and attention to detail. But again, not all.

And so I say to you, thirsty reader, that you do not need a passionate interest in all things Mennonite or mixology to enjoy this book. I will take you on a booze-soaked romp through the oddities of our history and culture. I will not bother you with pages upon pages detailing a comparison of various whiskies' flavour profiles. Nor will I bore you with lengthy disputations on theological justifications for one tenet of the faith or another. I will not even provide full and complete explanations of the various church schisms in our past. I do, however, encourage you to visit the companion blog, the Drunken Mennonite at slklassen.com, for all the fascinating details.

Because, after a few drinks, all of these stories will suddenly become absolutely riveting. Well, after quite a few drinks.

You might also be thinking that Mennonites do not drink alcoholic beverages—that we are such a morally upright faith group that we would spurn all things intoxicating. Here, too, you would be partially correct. There are some groups of Mennonites who, like other Christians around the turn of the 20th century, rejected the consumption of distilled beverages for a number of decades. Today, many of us have moved away from that prohibition, and the more conservative groups never accepted that prohibition in the first place. But there are still some holdouts.

The other reason you might imagine that Mennonites would be averse to cocktails is that it is a tenet of the Mennonite faith to keep in one way or another separate from the ways of the world. Not to worry. I have carefully designed the cocktails in this book to eschew worldliness. These are virtuous cocktails.

Ah, now I imagine you nodding, and it occurs to me that you may be a different kind of reader. Perhaps you are a Mennonite yourself. Or have a close connection to Mennonites.

In that case, you will have looked at this book with trepidation, wondering just how I have misrepresented your faith/ethnicity to the greater cocktail-book-reading public. You will approach the book with suspicion and prepare yourself to be disappointed in my lack of proper respect for the articles of faith and/or your own personal experience in your subgroup of the faith.

Such anxiety is, I am afraid, unavoidable.

Although I have worked hard to ensure that no Mennonites were harmed in the making of this book, I expect there will be a few who are dissatisfied. We have a reputation as a good and earnest people, and even the improper use of star anise in a cocktail may well cause a tsk here or there.

You will perhaps be mollified by the knowledge that my own Mennonite community has been surprisingly supportive of this whole endeavour. Or maybe that will just cause you to doubt the integrity of my congregation. It is true that the congregation allowed me full artistic licence on the condition that I provide them with mocktail recipes for their public gatherings. And cocktails for the private ones.

As you have probably surmised, my Mennonite community is of the so-called progressive variety. My people never dressed in a way to set themselves apart from those around them, and we adopted technological advances in much the same manner as our neighbours (though, perhaps, we were just a little bit grumpier about it). If you are of a different variety of Mennonite than me, then you may find yourself under-represented in this collection of thoughts and libations.

But I think you'll see yourself somewhere. Or, if not, I suggest that you open your mind to an Inter-Mennonite Drinking Experience. You might even find occasion to clink glasses with a cocktail aficionado who is not a Mennonite at all.

That is, if your congregation prayerfully discerns it to be okay.

I should warn you that this cocktail book lacks a few of the traditional elements of the Mennonite cookbook genre. Most notably, the book is entirely devoid of biblical quotes, inspirational aphorisms, and/or exhortations to live a better life. There aren't even any stories about how hospitality channels God's grace. Each recipe is accompanied by a short paragraph about the cocktail's connection to a Mennonite theme, but none of these paragraphs are even remotely inspirational. As a Mennonite reader/drinker, you may find this book just a tad frivolous. I suggest that you consume it in moderation.

Mennonite Cocktail Basics

As a people known to like hard work, Mennonites cannot endorse shortcuts in the making of cocktails. I expect you to squeeze your lemons and limes yourself and, ideally, use herbs grown in your own garden. Furthermore, as everything you do has ethical consequences, I encourage you to use fair trade and/or local ingredients whenever possible. When that is not possible, allow the guilt to wash over you. Don't worry, the pain doesn't last long.

Tools

Most Mennonites are raised to embrace frugality. Given this upbringing, it is difficult for me to justify purchasing a number of new tools and specialized glassware simply for making cocktails. I tried for months to make do with Mason jars, a paring knife, and a wooden spoon, but it turns out that a few good tools really are helpful.

Cocktail shaker. There are two kinds of shakers—the Boston shaker, which is like two large tumblers that fit together, and the cobbler cocktail shaker, which has a little strainer in the top and a cap. I suggest the latter because you can frugally avoid having to buy a separate strainer, and it is also easier to handle.

Mixing glass. These are pint-sized glasses with measurements along the sides that you use to make stirred (not shaken) cocktails. You do not really need one. A Mason jar, the bottom part of your cocktail shaker, or even a clean, empty pickle jar will do.

Cocktail strainer. Theoretically, you could use a kitchen sieve to strain your cocktails, but it is handy to have a Hawthorne strainer that sits nicely over the edge of your cocktail shaker.

Jigger. Jiggers are two-sided conical measuring tools that come in a variety of sizes. Seek out a jigger with 1 ounce (30 mL) on one side and ½ (15 mL) on the other. If it shows the ¼ ounce (7.5 mL) mark, even better. Otherwise, you will need to either buy another jigger that pairs 1¼ ounces (37.5 mL) with ¾ ounce (22 mL) or resort to measuring spoons. There's a handy conversion chart at the back of the book to help out if you want to measure with something other than a jigger. Some cobbler cocktail shakers not only have a built-in strainer but have caps ranging from ¾ to 1½ fluid ounces, some with markings. If you have one like that, congratulate yourself on your frugality and don't bother buying a jigger at all.

Muddler. This is a wide wooden stick used to smush up fruit, herbs, or spices. It functions like a pestle in a mortar and pestle. I used a wooden spoon for this and it works, but not as well.

Blender. Only a few cocktails require a blender. If you have one, make sure it is strong enough to crush ice. If not, you will need to crush ice in a bag or pillowcase with a hammer for those cocktails that require it. Do not use the hand-embroidered pillowcases that your grandmother made for you.

Bar spoon. A bar spoon is a long-handled spoon useful for mixing stirred cocktails and for floating (creating a layer of liquid at the top of a drink). Any long-handled spoon (like an iced-tea spoon) will also work.

Swizzle stick. A few cocktails want to be swizzled—this involves using a special stick that has blades at the end to cut through the crushed ice. Swizzling sounds very worldly, though, so don't worry about using a bar spoon or regular spoon instead.

Citrus juicer. Or you can just squeeze the lemons and limes and capture the juice in a bowl.

Zester. Seriously? It's not that hard getting the zest off a lemon or lime using a paring knife or a vegetable peeler.

Cocktail skewers. These are handy for holding garnishes in position. Avoid the ones fashioned to look like miniature swords as these are too militaristic for Mennonite mixology. In a pinch, you can also use a toothpick or even a large darning needle.

Ice cube trays. Don't think you can get away without ice. Splurge on a couple of trays at your local dollar or thrift store.

Glassware

You can serve your cocktails in any glasses that you like. Most Mennonite groups have a certain suspicion toward anything too fancy, and drinking from conical or hourglass-shaped vessels would certainly count as fancy. But if you happen to come upon a fancy cocktail glass at the local thrift shop or charity auction, it would be wrong not to use it. I have listed the glassware below, ranked from least to most worldly.

Old-fashioned glass, also known as a rocks glass. This glass is short and heavy. It is useful for strong drinks served on ice. It is also fine as an all-around useful kitchen glass. And with "old-fashioned" being in the name, this one can't be considered worldly at all.

Moscow mule mug. This copper mug could disguise itself as a camping cup. Because it is metal, it is indestructible and practical. Also, people have been drinking from copper cups for centuries, so this one has tradition on its side.

Highball. This is a tall glass that's used for cocktails that aren't quite so strong—cocktails that have juice or sparkling water. You might serve iced tea or even ice water in this glass on a hot day. It's a pretty functional glass. You may have one or two of them in your cupboard already without knowing it.

Shot glass. A shot glass is a little one-to-two-ounce glass that doubles as a toothpick holder in many a Mennonite household. Sounds reasonably unworldly.

Coupe glass. This glass has a shallow bowl on top of a stem and is good for many a small, shaken cocktail. It's a little fancy, but it's really just a fruit nappy on a stem. And the stem is useful to keep the heat of your hand from warming the beverage.

Julep cup. The traditional julep cup is an elegant sterling silver tumbler without a handle, often with decorative beading around the base. There's a certain worldliness to all that elegance. A stainless steel version is, however, a bit less worldly, especially if you put the glass to use to hold cut flowers or herbs when you are not enjoying a julep.

Flute glass. This is usually used for Champagne and other sparkling wines because it holds the bubbles. It is, however, a worldly glass. We should all remember that in the olden days, people were perfectly happy drinking Champagne from coupe glasses.

Martini glass. The epitome of fancy. A Mennonite uses this V-shaped glass only when they want to push the envelope on acceptable worldliness.

Hurricane glass. This is a very, very worldly glass. You can maybe use one of these for a margarita, but only if you received it as a gift or in a box at an auction that included many, much more sensible items.

Mennonite Flavours

While Mennonite communities live all around the world and eat the foods of their surroundings, two groups of Mennonites have developed food traditions with particular flavour profiles. Mennonites first migrated from Switzerland, the Alsace, and south Germany to North America in the 17th century and, together with other German Americans, developed what would become known as Pennsylvania Dutch cuisine. Known for the perhaps apocryphal axiom that all meals should have a balance of seven sweets and seven sours, the cocktails that honour this Mennonite tradition feature sweets and sours that are in homage to the jams and pickles that grace Pennsylvania Dutch tables.

Some of the more obscure flavours that crop up in this cocktail list reflect the cultural preferences of the Mennonites who sojourned in Eastern Europe. I have included savoury cocktails with notes of dill and sorrel in reference to these. The Mennonites who lived for a while in Russia have a penchant for the tartest of all plums, the damson. Many of those who continued on from Russia to Manitoba developed a passion for the powerfully bitter chokecherry. Good luck finding these items in your local grocery, but the quest is worth the effort. Some of the

Mennonites of this lineage ended up in Latin America and picked up yerba maté there. Rhubarb is loved by both ethnic groups of Mennonites. Until recently, we even had a literary magazine named after this weed-like stalk.

Ingredients and Substitutions

Frugality demands that we use what is already in our cupboards, and that means that you may sometimes wish to make some substitutions. Suggestions on how to convert a cocktail into a mocktail are listed at the end of the book in the "Sunday School Sippers" section. Apart from that, you should feel free to experiment. I have suggested triple sec for any of the cocktails that require an orange liqueur, but you can use Cointreau or even Grand Marnier if that is in your liquor cabinet. Maraschino liqueur and kirsch are both cherry flavoured, and in a pinch, you can substitute one for the other. When a recipe asks for aromatic bitters, you can use Angostura bitters (available in mainstream grocery stores) or homemade bitters as described in the "Syrups and Other Preserves" section at the end of the book. You'll end up with a different cocktail if you make any more significant alterations, but that's okay. We've never had any church schisms over lime versus lemon juice or bourbon versus rye. At least, not yet.

I have kept garnishes to a minimum in these recipes, lest the cocktails be considered too fancy for Mennonite consumption. Nonetheless, sometimes a garnish adds a small but significant flavour to the cocktail and is as much a part of the cocktail as the smallest child is a part of the congregation. See the garnish recipes in "Syrups and Other Preserves" at the end of the book to learn how to make citrus twists, pickled red onions, and cocktail cherries. (You could also substitute fresh or canned cherries for these homemade Boozy Maraschino Cherries.) For cocktails that do not call for a specific garnish, feel free to improvise with edible flowers, berries, and herbs from your garden. Store-bought is also okay, but only if you remember to bow your head and look appropriately ashamed for your gardening failure.

Mennonite Drinking Etiquette

Most of the recipes in this book provide measurements for one serving, but this does not mean that I am encouraging you to drink alone. Mennonites value fellowship, and fellowship requires two or more to be gathered together. If you want to prepare cocktails for more people than show up to rake the leaves at a church fall workday, flip to "Large-Quantity Cocktails" at the back. For smaller groups, I suggest making the cocktails one at a time.

You do not need to say grace or sing a hymn before enjoying cocktails with your friends, family, or deacons, but be aware that a toast raised by a Mennonite might come out sounding a lot like a prayer or a scripture reading of the Sermon on the Mount. It is perfectly acceptable to clink glasses to interrupt what seems like the start of a long-winded sermon. Just raise your glass and say, "To the peacemakers," and you should be fine.

We start our little drinking tour with a jaunt back in time to 16th-century Europe. There weren't actually cocktails then, but the good people of the time made up for this dearth of fun beverages by burning each other at the stake.

Not really.

Only a small proportion of the European population got burned at the stake, and even fewer Europeans actually started the blazes burning. But Mennonites look to the 16th-century Anabaptists as our spiritual ancestors, and they were the sort of people who got burned.

Anabaptists were some of the bit players of the massive religious movement in Europe called the Protestant Reformation. It was a time and a place where people really, really cared about stuff like baptism, divine judgment, and just how wrong everyone else was when they tried to interpret scripture.

Anabaptists were the ones that all the other reformers thought took things a step too far—by dangerously suggesting that baptism should be something chosen, not thrust upon one in infancy. Anabaptists fought over the right to baptize adults, and they died over it, never ever suspecting that we'd be making cocktails in their honour almost 500 years later.

PART I

ANABAPTIST IMBIBING

Death in the Age of Reform

Makes 1 cocktail

The first Anabaptists were born into a world that wasn't exactly medieval, but it sure as hell wasn't modern. Even if the population was starting to recover from the Black Death, more babies died as infants than grew to be adults. Those little ones existed in the blurry space between life and death, between spirit and flesh. And baptism—many people hoped—might keep the innocent ones safe from all the spiritually dangerous stuff out to get them. Even if they died.

Ernest Hemingway created the cocktail Death in the Afternoon sometime around 1935, but what did he know about death that these Europeans didn't already know in spades something like four centuries earlier? Here's to them. This variation uses the cheaper and more readily available Pernod instead of absinthe.

¼ oz (7.5 mL) Pernod
½ oz (15 mL) cold water
4 oz (125 mL) chilled sparkling wine

Mix the Pernod and the cold water in a small glass. It should become white and foggy. Pour into a champagne flute, and top with the sparkling wine. Imbibe while contemplating the brevity of life in the mists of time.

Poly-Gin-and-Juice

Makes 1 cocktail

About 50 years after a newfangled printing press started churning out Bibles, ordinary people started passing them around in the lands we now call Switzerland, Germany, and the Netherlands. Some of these new Bible-readers discovered that no babies were baptized in the Bible and suspected the practice of being ungodly. The idea of a social world without baptized babies branded these freethinkers as Enemies of the Social Order. And so the Friends of the Social Order called the radicals Anabaptists and imagined that they were one unified and nefarious group, when, in fact, our founders were many and disorganized—establishing what would become a 500-year tradition of Anabaptist disunity.

Polygenesis means "many beginnings." Poly-Gin-and-Juice has many juices. This is one of the easiest cocktails you'll ever make. You can use whatever juices you like. My recipe has cranberry and apple cider, but if you think that's too highfalutin, try whatever you want that is tart and simple. This is a drink for ordinary, disorganized folks, after all.

> 2 oz (60 mL) gin
> 2 oz (60 mL) apple cider (non-alcoholic)
> 1½ oz (45 mL) unsweetened cranberry juice

Pour the gin and juices into a mixing glass. Stir with ice until chilled. Strain. Make several of these, and serve over ice in a variety of old-fashioned glasses, each with its own unique origin story.

Brandy Anabaptist

Makes 2 cocktails

The first people to be called Anabaptist didn't claim the label for themselves. They didn't want to be known just for their stance on baptism, but that was what raised the ire of their neighbours, dukes, and emperor. They might not have minded if they'd been named the Adult Baptizers. But Anabaptist meant "rebaptizer," and that suggested that the first baptism—the one done to babies—worked and then the Anabaptists were redoing it. And maybe even cancelling out the first one in the process. Our reformers thought that baby baptism, at best, gave a false sense of certain salvation. At worst, well, you'd need a stiff drink to contemplate the horrors of the worst.

This cocktail is a variation of the Brandy Alexander, which combines brandy and cream. It's a small cocktail, and sweet. You might want to have it for dessert. This recipe makes two servings—I suggest having them both and arguing that the first one doesn't count.

> ½ cup (125 mL) whole or 2% milk
> ½ Tbsp (7.5 mL) white sugar
> 1 egg yolk
> A dash of vanilla extract
> 1½ oz (45 mL) brandy

Heat the milk and sugar in a small heavy pot until near boiling. Place the egg yolk in a mixing bowl, and add the hot milk, whisking to blend. Add a dash of vanilla. For a hot cocktail, add the brandy, and pour half into a serving cup and enjoy, saving the rest for your second round. For a cold version, chill the milk custard before adding the brandy, and serve in an old-fashioned glass over ice. Enjoy while considering the mysteries of birth, salvation, and custard.

Conrad Grebellini

Makes 1 cocktail

While many people were questioning the whole idea of baptizing newborns, only a couple of the questioners became famous for their efforts (not really famous—just famous among Mennonites). The story has it that in 1525, Conrad Grebel, Georg Blaurock, and Felix Manz were followers of Ulrich Zwingli, the church reformer in Zurich. These three, and maybe some of their unnamed friends, pushed Ulrich to ditch infant baptism. When Ulrich balked at the idea, they stormed off to Felix's mom's place and baptized each other. I bet Mrs. Manz served them drinks first.

Conrad Grebel was such a famous Anabaptist that we named a college after him in Waterloo, Ontario. And now a cocktail. A Bellini is a fizzy cocktail made with sparkling wine and peach purée. Those college students in Waterloo would probably like it. But they'll like it even more with a strawberry-rhubarb syrup that'll remind them of the classic pie flavours of their Mennonite childhoods.

> **2 oz (60 mL) strawberry-rhubarb syrup (see page 144), chilled**
> **4 oz (125 mL) chilled sparkling wine**

Measure the syrup into the bottom of a champagne flute or whatever glassware you are using. Top with the sparkling wine. Drink as a celebration of all our famous ancestors and the moms who hosted them.

Margret Hottingwallbanger

Makes 1 cocktail

Margret Hottinger was a famous Anabaptist back in the day. Honest. Just because no one's heard of her today doesn't mean she wasn't famous. She was arrested alongside Grebel, Manz, and Blaurock, so how's that for famous? She also preached and proselytized and gathered around her a following of other Anabaptist women. At least one of these women was, apparently, unorthodox enough to proselytize nude. Which is admittedly odd, even for us. And may have caused Margret the urge to bang her head against the wall. Or have a stiff drink.

The Harvey Wallbanger hails back to the 1970s when someone started floating a vanilla-flavoured liqueur on top of a screwdriver. Margret was living in nuttier times than the 1970s, so for this concoction, we are floating a nutty liqueur instead.

4 oz (125 mL) fresh orange juice
1½ oz (45 mL) vodka
½ oz (15 mL) amaretto

Mix the orange juice and vodka directly in an old-fashioned glass with ice. Float the amaretto on top by gently pouring the amaretto over the back of a bar spoon. Enjoy this cocktail with all your friends whether or not they have a penchant for proselytizing nude.

The German Peasants' Quaff

Makes 1 cocktail

When the peasants rebelled against their landlords in the German Peasants' War of 1525, all the major religious leaders denounced them. But not us. Well, let's face it. Even though we denied it later, some of us were peasant-Anabaptists ourselves and others were cheering the peasants on. Because saying no to baptizing babies in those days kinda meant saying no to the social hierarchy and our place in it. We paid for it afterward with the rulers of the land insisting that we were dangerous revolutionaries set to turn the world upside down. Which, to be fair, some of us were.

Ale would be the peasants' drink of choice in the lands where those who may or may not have been influenced by Anabaptism rebelled against the rich and powerful. But this take on a shandy is fine enough for noble and peasant to enjoy together.

1¼ oz (37.5 mL) fresh lemon juice
1½ oz (45 mL) simple syrup (see page 141)
10–12 frozen raspberries
4–5 oz (125–150 mL) ale (use a pale or amber ale)

Mix together the lemon juice and simple syrup directly in a highball glass. Add the raspberries and the beer. Bottoms up to all those at the bottom of the social hierarchy struggling to turn the world upside down.

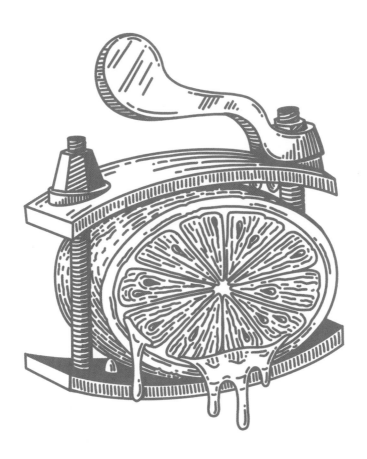

Thumbscrew Driver

Nothing says a Mennonite history lesson quite like a catalogue of 16th-century instruments of torture. One of our favourite picture books is called *The Bloody Theater, or Martyrs Mirror of the Defenseless Christians: Who Baptized Only upon Confession of Faith, and Who Suffered and Died for the Testimony of Jesus, Their Saviour, from the Time of Christ to the Year A.D. 1660.* The title of the book is torturous enough, but it is also bedecked with 104 illustrations of torture and martyrdom. Sometimes torture was supposed to entice Anabaptists to recant. Other times, it was hoped that torture would loosen their tongues so they'd name their fellows and the locations of their leaders.

This cocktail is far less painful than the thumbscrew but, if applied correctly and in copious amounts, might on occasion loosen a tongue or two as well. Since we're still kinda bitter about the whole century of torture, this version of a screwdriver includes the bitter orange Campari liqueur.

> 2 oz (60 mL) vodka
> ½ oz (15 mL) Campari
> 4 oz (125 mL) fresh orange juice
> An orange twist (see page 147) to garnish

Combine all ingredients except the garnish directly in an old-fashioned glass and serve over ice. Garnish with an orange twist, using an instrument of torture to squeeze a bit of oil from the twist into the cocktail if you are so inclined. Drink carefully, guarding your tongue lest the cocktail weaken your resolve.

The Schleitside

Makes 1 cocktail

In 1527, when Anabaptism was still a wee confessional unbaptized baby, a group of men who fancied themselves its leaders got together in the town of Schleitheim. There, they drew up the Schleitheim Confession—a document that listed seven articles of faith that they all agreed upon. Never mind all the other Anabaptists who didn't agree. The Schleitheim Confession is one of our foundational documents and has the honour of being the first of many documents to sow disagreement among Anabaptists.

The Schleitside cocktail takes its inspiration from a minty gin cocktail called a Southside. To honour the Schleitheim Confession, this cocktail muddles exactly seven mint leaves; one for each article. Feel free to disagree about them.

> 7 fresh mint leaves, plus a sprig of mint to garnish
> 2 oz (60 mL) gin
> ¾ oz (22 mL) simple syrup (see page 141)
> ¾ oz (22 mL) fresh lime juice
> A dash of elderflower liqueur
> A dash of absinthe or star anise bitters (see page 148)

Place the mint in the bottom of a cocktail shaker, and add the gin. Muddle to release the mint flavours, and then add the other ingredients except for the garnish. Fill the shaker halfway with ice, and shake thoroughly. Strain into a coupe glass, or serve over ice in a highball glass. Garnish with mint. Sip this cocktail while preparing your own laundry list of things to believe.

Münstirred Cocktail

Makes 1 cocktail

For 16 glorious and bizarre months, Anabaptists held power in the city of Münster. At least, people say they were bizarre. We don't really know because when the evil bishop of Waldeck and his army took back the city, he didn't leave a single friendly witness alive. And so all we have are unsubstantiated rumours of sex and violence. But it doesn't matter. Mennonites have accepted them as true and have been ashamed of our days in Münster ever since. In fact, we'll often deny having any kinship whatsoever with the Münster Anabaptists. Just see if you can get a Mennonite to drink to them.

This cocktail uses a fortified wine in honour of Münster's fortifications. Because there is no way that a ragtag group of Anabaptists could have held off an army for 16 months without them.

2 oz (60 mL) rye whisky
1 oz (30 mL) ruby port
1 tsp (5 mL) maraschino liqueur

Pour all ingredients into a mixing glass. Stir with ice until well chilled. Strain into a coupe glass, or serve on ice in an old-fashioned glass. This is a strong drink; feel the burn of misrepresentation in your throat even as the power in the beverage stokes the fire in your belly.

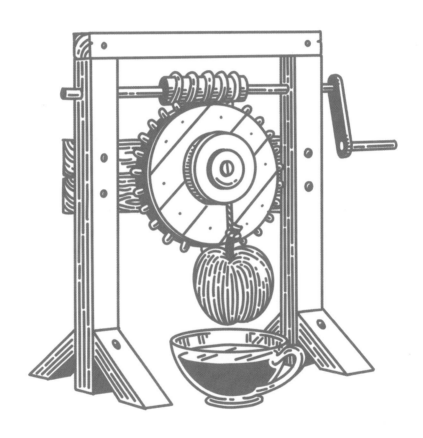

Pilgram Marpunch

Makes 1 cocktail

Pilgram Marpeck was a 16th-century engineer. Just like Leonardo da Vinci. If Leonardo had been an Anabaptist and had a sideline in theology instead of art, then he could have been Pilgram Marpeck's twin. The evil twin. We all know that Pilgram was the better of the two men. Pilgram was steadfastly opposed to violence and coercion, whereas Leonardo designed war machines.

This cocktail pays tribute to the apple trees of the Tyrol region, where Pilgram spent his youth. It is easily made in large batches, so you can prepare enough for a whole subversive community of Anabaptists in hiding.

> 1 oz (30 mL) gold rum
> ¼ oz (7.5 mL) triple sec
> ½ oz (15 mL) apple cider (non-alcoholic)
> ½ oz (15 mL) English breakfast tea, brewed and chilled
> A slice of apple to garnish

Pour all ingredients except the garnish into a mixing glass. Stir with ice until chilled, and strain into a coupe glass or punch cup. Garnish with an apple slice, and drink somewhere far away from the machines of war, knowing that coercion is never a good strategy in life or cocktails.

Menno Sidecar

Makes 1 cocktail

Let's get this straight. Menno Simons was no one's founder. He wrote some good sermons and brought together a lot of peace-loving Anabaptists who, like him, were embarrassed about the whole debacle at Münster, but none of them asked that we be named after him. It's just that so many people kept calling us after him that eventually we got tired of correcting them and so went with it. We've been called worse.

According to legend, Menno Simons once fell into a barrel of molasses while hurrying to escape prosecution. This variation of a sidecar uses molasses simple syrup.

> **2 oz (60 mL) brandy**
> **½ oz (15 mL) triple sec**
> **½ oz (15 mL) fresh lemon juice, plus more for the rim**
> **½ oz (15 mL) molasses simple syrup (see page 142)**

Rim a coupe glass with sugar by dipping the glass in lemon juice and then in sugar. Add all ingredients to a cocktail shaker filled halfway with ice. Shake until chilled. Strain into the prepared glass. Enjoy your beverage—don't worry if you're not a fan of its name.

Strasbourbon

Makes 1 cocktail

When all the other towns and principalities were busy accusing Anabaptists of trying to uproot the very basis of society, Strasbourg took no heed and welcomed us in. At its peak, 2 out of every 15 Strasbourgians were reputed to have been Anabaptists. Which is almost as many as you'd find today at a thrift store bargain bin. But then the Strasbourg leaders discovered that the Anabaptists really did want to turn society upside down. And so they kicked us out. Here's to the memories, Strasbourg.

This is a crowd-pleasing cocktail following a classic formula. It's a bit like a whiskey sour but it's red, like the blood of the martyrs apprehended when forced to flee our so-called Refuge of Righteousness.

> 1½ oz (45 mL) bourbon
> ½ oz (15 mL) triple sec
> ¼ oz (7.5 mL) unsweetened cranberry juice

Pour all ingredients into a mixing glass. Stir with ice. Strain into a coupe or martini glass. Drink boldly, with the righteous anger of one who has unjustly been cast from their home.

Bloody Martyr

Makes 1 cocktail

If you hear someone telling you not to be a martyr, then you can be pretty sure that the speaker is not a Mennonite. We Mennonites love our martyrs. And we've got lots of them. We figure that over 4,000 Anabaptists were put to death between 1525 and 1600 for refusing to recant and turn back to the state church. We haven't had as many since then, but that's not for want of trying. You know what they say—the blood of the martyr is the inspiration for a cocktail.

This cocktail is based on a Bloody Mary. It's a pleasant low-alcohol beverage that goes well with brunch—that late-morning meal one eats after having already put in six hours of early-morning labour.

3 oz (90 mL) tomato juice
1½ oz (45 mL) vodka
1½ oz (45 mL) pickle juice
¾ oz (22 mL) Worcestershire sauce
½ tsp (2.5 mL) prepared horseradish
5–6 dashes hot sauce
A pinch of fresh dill
A small dill pickle or dill floret to garnish

Mix all ingredients except the garnish directly in a highball glass, and serve over ice. Garnish with a pickle or dill floret. Face down this cocktail with the calm resolve of one who knows they are drinking a cocktail that is righteous to the end.

Maeyken's Boozy Milkshake

Makes 1 cocktail

When Maeyken Boosers was in prison in 1564, her little son visited and she gave him a pear. Perhaps she thought he looked a little peckish. Perhaps she didn't really like pears, or perhaps she just couldn't stomach to eat the pear herself so close before her execution. She no doubt expected him to eat it. But the boy didn't eat it and neither did his heirs or theirs after them, and now a dried and thoroughly rotten pear sits in the Amsterdam archives in remembrance of an Anabaptist woman and her son who didn't want to eat it.

This cocktail is a milkshake to satisfy the inner child-who-refuses-to-eat-the-food-set-before-them in all of us. It works well with chocolate or caramel ice cream.

3 scoops ice cream
4 oz (125 mL) whole or 2% milk
1 oz (30 mL) gold rum
1 oz (30 mL) pear liqueur or pear brandy
1 pear

Start by putting the ice cream in a blender. Add the milk, rum, and pear liqueur or brandy. Blend just until mixed. Serve a pear alongside the cocktail, but do not even consider eating it—the pear is to be saved for posterity.

Dirk 'n' Willemsy

Makes 1 cocktail

Dirk Willems is everyone's favourite Anabaptist hero. It wasn't enough for him to just get martyred. Oh, no. *Anyone* could get themselves killed for being an Anabaptist in the 16th century. By the 1560s, that was old hat. But Dirk showed up all the run-of-the-mill Anabaptist martyrs by turning back during his daring escape to rescue the bailiff who was pursuing him and who had fallen through some thin ice. That act assured Dirk's capture and death but also his immortality in Mennonite memory as the ultimate "love of enemies" guy.

We can't all be Dirk Willems, but we can all enjoy this riff on the Dark 'n' Stormy.

3 oz (90 mL) gold rum
1 oz (30 mL) fresh lime juice
½ oz (15 mL) ginger syrup (see page 143)
2 oz (60 mL) ginger beer

Pour the rum, lime juice, and ginger syrup directly into a highball glass with ice. Stir and top with the ginger beer. Sip on a mild day in winter when the ice is just beginning to crack up, and don't forget to offer a glass to your enemy, should one come along as you are imbibing.

The Baroness von Freyberg

Makes 1 cocktail

Not all of us died martyred deaths. People like Helena von Freyberg recanted just to get out of prison and then went back to their seditious Anabaptist ways. Helena became an important leader in Augsburg after her release. But as far as we can tell, she never managed to stop feeling guilty about her failure to be martyred.

This cocktail is based on the non-alcoholic Baroness Cocktail, but it adds some gin. You can have the alcoholic version and then recant and have the other by just leaving out the gin. It's okay, really.

> **2 oz (60 mL) pear juice**
> **1½ oz (45 mL) gin**
> **½ oz (15 mL) fresh lemon juice**
> **¼ oz (7.5 mL) ginger syrup (see page 143)**

Pour all ingredients into a cocktail shaker filled halfway with ice. Shake thoroughly, and strain into a martini glass. Enjoy the cocktail, resigned to the knowledge that you, too, may never experience martyrdom.

Let us digress a little now from the relentless flow of history and relax with a drink in one hand and a religious tract in the other. Not a real religious tract—don't worry. Mennonites are not big into handing out tracts. But you can imagine the little blurbs above each recipe here as the text you might find in a tract that outlines some of our tenets of faith. This will save you, poor reader, from needing to read hefty tomes of theology and hermeneutics to understand us.

But because religion is important in the Mennonite identity—even for those who no longer attend church services—a drinking tour through the Mennonite world must include a certain amount of theology.

The following cocktails reference some of the (always disputed) tenets of faith that are common to the people who practise the Mennonite faith. We are a people who consider ourselves followers of Jesus, using the scriptures in the Bible as a guide.

Apart from that, there is little that all different groupings of Mennonites agree upon.

One thing we (mostly) hold in common is that faith is enacted in daily life. If cocktails are part of daily life, then faith is, ergo, enacted through cocktails. If cocktails are not part of everyday life, I ask you, why not?

PART II

FAITH
AND
LIBATIONS

The Peaceable Gimlet

Makes 1 cocktail

Mennonites have been opposed to state violence since before there were nation-states. We've never been very popular when our countries went to war, and usually get really uncomfortable at the sound of patriotic jingoism. Several of our churches and plenty of individual Mennonites have dropped or modified the peace position at various points in history, but we don't focus on that. Most of us today hold fast to pacifism and non-violence and measure courage by the strength of our resolve to evade army recruiters.

This cocktail is as traditional as the Mennonite peace position. A gimlet is essentially a gin sour made with sweetened lime juice, and its history goes way back (not to before there were nation-states, but close enough). I suggest adding a few drops of rhubarb bitters if you have them. If you don't, no sweat. It's nothing worth fighting over.

> 2 oz (60 mL) gin
> ¾ oz (22 mL) fresh lime juice
> ¾ oz (22 mL) rhubarb syrup (see page 144)
> A dash of rhubarb bitters (see page 148) (optional)
> A lime wedge and/or cocktail cherry (see page 147) to garnish

Pour all ingredients except the garnish into a cocktail shaker filled halfway with ice. Shake until chilled. Strain into a coupe glass, and garnish with lime and/or a cherry. Sip this cocktail with the courage of your convictions, remembering that *pacifist* does not mean "passive."

Upon Confession of Fizz

Makes 1 cocktail

For all we disagree about many things, all Mennonites agree with our Anabaptist ancestors that joining the church involves an adult declaration or "confession" of faith. Or maybe an adolescent confession of faith. Or maybe a late-childhood confession of faith. Whatever. Just a confession of faith.

This is an adult beverage, but there's no need to declare anything before enjoying this version of a gin fizz.

> 1½ oz (45 mL) gin
> 1 oz (30 mL) rhubarb syrup (see page 144)
> ½ oz (15 mL) fresh lemon juice
> 1 egg white (optional)
> Sparkling water to top

Pour all ingredients except sparkling water in a cocktail shaker. If using egg white, shake thoroughly without ice until frothy, lifting the lid occasionally to allow air to escape. (Skip this step if not using egg white.) Add some ice and shake until chilled. Pour into a highball glass, and top with sparkling water. Gulp this down as a mark of your faith in the pleasures of gin and rhubarb, whether or not you feel inclined to confess it.

Mode of Baptiki

Makes 1 cocktail

We've been bickering and breaking up congregations for centuries over the mode of baptism—if we should sprinkle a bit of water, pour a bit more from a pitcher, or totally immerse the baptizee into a pool or river. Mennonites see baptism not as a rite that washes away original sin, but rather as a symbol of our commitment to a life following Christ as a member of the congregation. But just because it's a symbol doesn't mean it's not important enough to fight over.

This cocktail won't end the strife, but it offers a tribute to each of the three major modes (pouring, immersing, and sprinkling). Tiki cocktails are cocktails that feature tropical fruits and often rum. They're not symbolic of anything.

2 oz (60 mL) gold rum
¾ oz (22 mL) triple sec
1 oz (30 mL) fresh orange juice
1 oz (30 mL) pineapple juice
A piece of pineapple and a cocktail cherry (see page 147)
A dash of aromatic bitters

Pour all ingredients except the bitters into a cocktail shaker filled halfway with ice. Shake thoroughly until chilled, and strain into a martini glass. Secure the cocktail cherry to the pineapple piece with a cocktail stick or a toothpick, and immerse it into the cocktail. Sprinkle with bitters. Drink confidently in the knowledge that this cocktail will wash away whatever needs to be cleansed.

CPT: Crimson Peachwater Tea

Makes 1 cocktail

The Christian Peacemaker Teams are Mennonites and other activist Christians who seek to dismantle the structures of oppression through creative non-violence all around the world. Progressive Mennonites love CPT. We all have CPTers in our networks of friends and family. And usually also former CPTers who were kicked out or left in a huff. For reasons unclear to all of us. This drink's for all of them—the heroes and the victims of peacemaking.

This cocktail asks you to walk alongside people suffering from systems of oppression and share a cup of tea. And something just a little stronger.

1 oz (30 mL) peach schnapps
½ oz (15 mL) Campari
¾ oz (22 mL) English breakfast tea, brewed and chilled

Pour all ingredients into a mixing glass, and stir with ice until chilled. Strain into an old-fashioned glass and serve over ice. Raise a glass to the heroism of peacemaking.

The Community of Juleps

Makes 1 cocktail

In every Mennonite crowd, there's always at least one person who will break up any party by reminding us that we all should really be practising the *community of goods*, like (some of) our 16th-century ancestors. They mean that we shouldn't have rich and poor but should all pool our resources. The Hutterites—who are also Anabaptists, but not Mennonites—do that and live communally. Mennonites never really have. If you meet such a buzzkill, I suggest a humble nod in agreement and an offer to share a drink.

This cocktail is a mint julep, deepened with the rich flavour of brown sugar—be sure that this richness is equitably shared about in the cocktail.

2 oz (60 mL) bourbon
¾ oz (22 mL) mint brown sugar syrup (see page 143)
Crushed ice to serve

Combine the bourbon and syrup in a mixing glass. Fill a julep cup or old-fashioned glass with crushed ice, and pour the bourbon and syrup overtop. Make enough of these to share and serve in solidarity with the economically disadvantaged.

True Frangelico Faith

Makes 1 cocktail

Menno Simons once said, "True evangelical faith does not lie dormant. It clothes the naked and feeds the poor." It goes on but this is the famous part and at least one in a hundred Mennonites know it by heart. It is also the only piece of Menno Simons's writings that anyone at all knows by heart. And that's really just because someone put the lines to music and made a hymn out of it. We sing it every time we want to feel guilty about not doing enough for the poor and needy.

This is a simple cocktail that will not divert too much of your time from comforting the sorrowful and sheltering the destitute.

> **4 oz (125 mL) whole or 2% milk**
> **2 oz (60 mL) Frangelico**
> **A dash of chocolate bitters (see page 148)**

Pour the milk and Frangelico directly into an old-fashioned glass. Top with the bitters. Stir with ice. Drink down while planning all the good works you will do tomorrow. Or sometime.

Mulled Witness

Makes 8 servings

For some Mennonites, witnessing their faith to others means evangelizing, and for others it means doing good in the world as an example to others. Some of us don't do any of that. Some used to evangelize and now look back on that period as an embarrassing colonial project. Others think those Mennonites have fallen away and forgotten the call to speak the Word of God to all peoples. This isn't something we can ever agree upon. But there's a lot to mull over.

While there is much to mull around all year, mulled wine is traditionally a winter drink.

    1 bottle (24 oz/750 mL) fruit-forward red wine
    ½ cup (125 mL) unsweetened cranberry juice
    ⅓ cup (80 mL) mulling syrup (see page 144)
    Fresh or frozen cranberries

Combine the wine, cranberry juice, and syrup in a pot, and place over medium heat until hot. Add the cranberries and serve in teacups or mugs. Consume consciously as a model of moderate consumption, and then go forth and proclaim the goodness of this beverage to all creation.

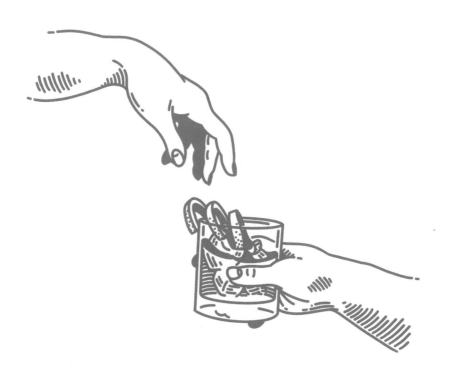

Old Freundschaft

Makes 1 cocktail

The word *Freundschaft* literally means friendship and amity, or group of friends and family. It's an essential building block of community. Mennonites are individualistic in that the choice to join the church is an individual one, but we're also pretty communitarian. Sometimes that goes off in a mystical "the Holy Spirit speaks through community discernment" direction, and sometimes it just means we get together for a lot of potlucks and quilting bees.

This cocktail riffs off the classic old-fashioned. I wouldn't suggest it for a huge communal gathering like a wedding or a barn raising, but it's good for when it's just the freundschaft, and there's a bottle of bourbon on hand.

¼ oz (7.5 mL) molasses simple syrup (see page 142)
1½ oz (45 mL) bourbon
2 dashes aromatic bitters
An orange twist (see page 147) to garnish

Pour the syrup directly into the bottom of an old-fashioned glass, and add bourbon. Stir with ice until thoroughly chilled. Add the bitters, and squeeze the orange twist over the drink to draw out just a bit of the oils, and then drop the whole thing into the cocktail. Sip gently and allow the strength of the bourbon to ease the existential angst of being an individual with volition in a group guided by the apparent hand of God.

Mutual (Lemon) Aid

Makes 1 cocktail

It is often said that if a barn burns down in a Mennonite community, all of the neighbours will come together to help rebuild it. This is really just true among the Amish (who aren't really Mennonite) and the Old Order Mennonites (who are). As most Mennonites live in cities now, there isn't a lot of call for barn raisings among progressive Mennonites. But we're still pretty taken with the idea of mutual aid and have been known to help each other with casseroles and financial assistance on occasion.

This vodka lemonade cocktail is the perfect drink to accompany a barn raising or any other reason to get together with neighbours. Be warned that you would need to make a lot of these for an actual barn raising. (And for a list of other cocktails that would be suitable in large quantities, see page 139.)

1 oz (30 mL) vodka
¾ oz (22 mL) green Chartreuse
1 oz (30 mL) fresh lemon juice
½ oz (15 mL) fresh orange juice
½ oz (15 mL) simple syrup (see page 141)
2 oz (60 mL) sparkling water

Fill a highball glass with crushed ice or ice cubes. Combine all ingredients in a mixing glass, adding the sparkling water last. Pour over the ice in the prepared glass, or make a pitcher to serve to your friends and neighbours while they pitch in to help rebuild whatever needs rebuilding.

Let Your Yes Be a Yes
and Your No Mojito

Makes 1 cocktail

Mennonites don't swear oaths. If you get one of us up on the witness stand and put a Bible under our hand, we will refuse to swear anything. Which must be annoying to everyone just trying to do their jobs in a criminal justice system that thinks hands on Bibles matter. It's not that Mennonites don't think that the Bible matters. It's just that there are a couple of lines in it telling us not to swear on anything and just to let our yes be a yes and our no, no. And we're just like that.

This cocktail is a refreshing accompaniment to a summer potluck and is low enough in alcohol that you shouldn't have to worry about getting tipsy and bursting out in inappropriate hymn sings. Well, I wouldn't swear to that.

> 1 lime, in quarters
> 8–10 fresh mint leaves
> ½ oz (15 mL) simple syrup (see page 141)
> 1½ oz (45 mL) white rum
> A dash of aromatic bitters
> 4 oz (125 mL) sparkling water
> Crushed ice to serve

Squeeze some of the juice out of the lime, and add it, the lime quarters, and the mint directly to a highball glass. Muddle gently to release the mint and lime flavours. Add the simple syrup, rum, and bitters and mix well. Add crushed ice and sparkling water. Stir gently with a swizzle stick or long-handled spoon. Drink with pleasure, and feel free to affirm (but not swear to) its goodness to all your fellow tipplers.

Nonconformopolitan

Makes 1 cocktail

One of the articles of the Schleitheim Confession warns us against conforming to the ways of the world. Sure, the Bible said it first, but it went on to talk about renewing the mind, and the Schleitheim Confession instead talked about abomination, which is much more exciting. It's never been entirely clear which parts of the world are the worldly parts, but I'm betting that neither Paul nor the early Anabaptists were thinking about fruity vodka cocktails at the time. Which means this is fine.

Worldly Cosmopolitans use sweetened cranberry juice, but we are turning our backs on that and using the non-conforming unsweetened cranberry and a measure of minty simple syrup for a fresh start.

> 1½ oz (45 mL) vodka
> ½ oz (15 mL) triple sec
> ¾ oz (22 mL) unsweetened cranberry juice
> ½ oz (15 mL) fresh lime juice
> ½ oz (15 mL) mint brown sugar syrup (see page 143)

Pour all ingredients into a cocktail shaker filled halfway with ice. Shake until chilled. Strain into a coupe or martini glass. Imbibe on your own or with a few friends, content in your choice and satisfied in the knowledge that you have prevailed against the pressures to conform to the ways of the ungodly world.

Plainoma

Makes 1 cocktail

Many people think that all Mennonites dress "plain"—this is why they confuse us with the Amish and the Quaker Oats guy. And a few Mennonite groups do dress plain, to avoid vanity and conforming to the ways of the fashion world. Most of us, however, manage to be unfashionable without making it a tenet of our faith.

This is a plain version of a paloma. No fancy grapefruit soda pop in this cocktail.

2 oz (60 mL) tequila
1½ oz (45 mL) fresh grapefruit juice
½ oz (15 mL) fresh lime juice
½ oz (15 mL) simple syrup (see page 141)
3 oz (90 mL) sparkling water

Combine ingredients except for the sparkling water in a cocktail shaker with ice. Shake thoroughly and strain into a highball glass with ice. Top with sparkling water. Enjoy in a spirit of humility, and do not even think of putting a fancypants garnish on the edge of this cocktail's glass.

Fancy Navel

Makes 1 cocktail

Plain Mennonites will sometimes call Mennonites who don't dress plain "fancy." It's not a compliment. There is not a branch of the Mennonite Church that aspires to "fancy" nor a congregation that would feel anything but slighted were its church interior called fancy. But so what? If you want to call us fancy, that's fine. We'll just be sitting here enjoying a sweet little cocktail that's a bit too fancy for the more humble among us.

A Fuzzy Navel is a fun little drink that was popular out in the world in the 1980s. This version adds a bit of Chambord and some sparkling wine to make it even fancier. Feel free to sub in your own homemade raspberry cordial if Chambord is a bit too fancy for you.

> 2 oz (60 mL) fresh orange juice
> 1 oz (30 mL) peach schnapps
> ½ oz (15 mL) Chambord
> 2 oz (60 mL) chilled sparkling wine
> A dash of aromatic bitters
> Orange wedges, cocktail cherries (see page 147), and/or edible flowers to garnish

Make this cocktail in the fanciest glass that you own. Start by mixing the first 3 ingredients directly in the bottom of the glass. Add ice and then top with sparkling wine. Throw in a dash of aromatic bitters just because you can, and top with an elaborate garnish made from orange wedges, cherries, and/or edible flowers. Drink nonchalantly, coolly ignoring all passive-aggressive comments of judgment from your peers.

A Glass of Gelassenheit

Makes 1 cocktail

Gelassenheit means "yieldedness" and refers to that feeling that comes from giving up your individual will to the collectively discerned will of God. It is a concept dear to many of the more conservative branches of the Mennonite faith and sometimes admired by the progressives. Especially when we can't find enough volunteers to wash the dishes after a potluck or rake the leaves around the church.

This cocktail has not been collectively discerned as the will of God, but it has been tested and collectively discerned to be delicious.

> 1 cucumber
> 2 oz (60 mL) gin
> ½ oz (15 mL) fresh lemon juice
> ½ oz (15 mL) rhubarb syrup (see page 144)
> Sparkling water to top (optional)

Draw a vegetable peeler along the length of the cucumber to make 2 or 3 long, wide ribbons. Wrap the cucumber ribbons around the inside of an old-fashioned glass. Add ice to hold the cucumber ribbons in place. In a cocktail shaker, combine the gin, lemon juice, and rhubarb syrup. Shake vigorously and strain into the prepared glass. Top with sparkling water for a lighter cocktail. Enjoy, giving yourself over completely to the herbaceous goodness of gin, rhubarb, and cucumber.

Shunned and Banned

Makes 1 cocktail

Long before social media, Mennonites had our own cancel culture. And we were really good at it. We didn't just unfriend each other one by one; we institutionalized social ostracism. Some Mennonites called it the Ban, some called it Shunning, and some just called it Church Discipline. Whatever we called it, it always involved cancelling someone by ignoring their existence. Thankfully, no one has ever been disciplined for making silly puns and spoonerisms out of cocktail names. Yet.

This cocktail is a variation of the Blood and Sand, a classic cocktail that uses Scotch whisky—a spirit usually shunned from cocktail recipes.

¾ oz (22 mL) blended Scotch
¾ oz (22 mL) brandy
¾ oz (22 mL) kirsch
¾ oz (22 mL) fresh orange juice
An orange twist (see page 147) to garnish

Pour all ingredients except the garnish into a cocktail shaker with ice. Shake and strain into a coupe or martini glass. Garnish with an orange twist, and dare the church elders to find a rule against Scotch cocktails. Drink like nobody's watching—which would be true if they have already placed you under the Ban and are not allowed to watch.

(French) 75-Minute Service

Makes 1 cocktail

Back in the 20th century, Mennonite church services in progressive churches were 60 minutes—no longer, no shorter. It was a rule and people respected it. But we have grown sloppy in our timekeeping, and the services have grown longer. Seventy-five minutes is now an acceptable norm, and that does not even include the singing of hymns before the service begins or the chatting over coffee afterward. Weddings are sometimes shorter. Funerals are longer. This is just the way things are now.

Fortunately, there's a lovely little cocktail with the number 75 in its name. It's a pleasant beverage, as comfy as a padded pew. But be careful—the gin will hit you like the admonitions of a pulpit-thumping preacher if you have more than one of these easy-drinking tipples.

1½ oz (45 mL) gin
¾ oz (22 mL) fresh lemon juice
¾ oz (22 mL) brown sugar syrup (see page 142)
3 oz (90 mL) chilled sparkling wine

Mix the gin, lemon juice, and syrup directly in the bottom of a champagne flute or coupe glass. Top with sparkling wine. Sip slowly and watch the minutes fly by.

Four-Part Sangria

Makes 8 servings

Mennonites are known around the world for our prowess as four-part harmony hymn singers (except for those of us who think it is worldly and only sing in unison). Some theories attribute our love of hymn singing to the repression of all other forms of pleasure; others claim that harmonious singing is a way to compensate for the disharmony in our personal relationships. Whatever the cause, children raised in the Mennonite faith typically learn to sing harmony even before they can sit through a sermon. By the time we reach adolescence, we are so steeped in hymn singing that we are universally recognized as eccentric among our non-Mennonite peers and have no hope of a normal life.

Four-Part Sangria features four ingredients in perfect harmony. Unlike Mennonites who can burst into song at a moment's notice, the ingredients in this sangria need to sit together for a number of hours before they are in perfect harmony.

> **About 3 cups (750 mL) seasonal fruit, chopped**
> **4 oz (125 mL) triple sec**
> **2 oz (60 mL) kirsch**
> **1 bottle (24 oz/750 mL) fruit-forward red wine**

Put fruit in the bottom of a large pitcher. If the fruit is tart, add some sugar and stir. Pour the triple sec and kirsch over the fruit, and let sit for a few hours. Add the wine and chill thoroughly. Serve over ice in wineglasses, and distribute among your guests after they have arranged themselves with sopranos on the right, altos on the left, and tenors and basses behind them.

Congregational Swizzle

Makes 1 cocktail

Mennonites have no pope or central hierarchy setting out the tenets of faith and rules for living. Instead, among most groups, individual congregations do what they want without worrying about a district or national or international governing body stepping in and causing trouble. Which is all fun and games until some congregation goes awry. But never mind about them.

    This cocktail is based on the Queen's Park Swizzle, which is built in the glass, one ingredient on top of the next. No one—or at least no one outside of your congregation—will judge you if you substitute mint for the ginger syrup or even leave out the mint entirely.

> 4–5 fresh mint leaves, plus more to garnish
> ½ oz (15 mL) ginger syrup (see page 143)
> 2 oz (60 mL) white rum
> ¾ oz (22 mL) fresh lime juice
> Crushed ice to serve
> 4–5 dashes (1 tsp/5 mL) aromatic bitters

Muddle the mint leaves with the ginger syrup directly in the bottom of a highball glass. Add the rum and lime juice. Fill the glass half to three-quarters full of crushed ice. Stir with a swizzle stick or long-handled spoon until chilled. Fill the glass to the top with more ice, and top with aromatic bitters. Garnish with more mint leaves. Serve with a straw (or spoon) in the presence of your congregation, not caring a whit if another congregation disapproves.

Despite rumours to the contrary, faithful reader, Mennonites have not actually stayed the same from the 16th century to the present but, instead, continued to exist in history from the 17th century onward. As such, we have been part of all the big sweeping historical trends that made the modern world.

Not that we noticed. We were typically too busy to pay much attention. Too busy either fighting among ourselves or trying to decide whether it was time to move on again. And so, yes, we participated in the social and economic and political movements that defined the modern age—we had our share of industrialists and institution builders—we just didn't care that much.

As a result, the following cocktails reference key moments in our schismatic and migratory history. If you want to know about the big sweeping trends that made the modern world, you will have to look for a "History of World Civilizations Cocktail Book."

PART III

MOVED BY THE SPIRITS

Migratarita

Makes 1 cocktail

Whenever Mennonites aren't happy where we are, we up and leave. We've migrated for various reasons. Because of religious persecution or the land was crappy where we were or we suspected the government of wanting to interfere in our schools or whatever. Mostly, we like to think of it all as religious persecution. These days, there's talk of a migration into space.

This cocktail is for all of the times that Mennonites migrated, and might migrate in the future. We just need to make sure we go somewhere with tequila.

> 2 oz (60 mL) tequila
> 1 oz (30 mL) triple sec
> ¼ cup (60 mL) watermelon purée (or heaping ⅓ cup/80 mL frozen
> watermelon cubes)
> 1 oz (30 mL) fresh lime juice
> ½ oz (15 mL) simple syrup (see page 141)

Pour all ingredients into a cocktail shaker, and shake thoroughly with ice. Serve in a coupe or martini glass. For a frozen version, use frozen watermelon, and blend everything together in a blender. Take a sip and see if it's to your liking. If not, move somewhere with better watermelon-growing conditions.

Frisian Bluster

Makes 1 cocktail

Flemish Mennonites fled in the late 16th century to Friesland, where they took an almost instant dislike to the Frisian Mennonites who were already there. The two groups set off the most epic of all Mennonite schisms with a dispute over, among other things, whether it was better to read sermons that had been written earlier or just speak off the cuff. It was a long and cruel schism, and if you know how to look, you can still see its impact in the services of some of the separatist Mennonite groups in Canada and Latin America.

Neither of the factions proposed sermons by filibuster—the name of the cocktail on which this one is based—though an outsider could be forgiven for not noticing the difference. If you don't want to read the recipe, go ahead and whip this cocktail up however the spirit moves you.

1½ oz (45 mL) rye whisky
½ oz (15 mL) fresh lemon juice
½ oz (15 mL) maple syrup
1 egg white
A dash of unsweetened cranberry juice
A dash of aromatic bitters

Pour all ingredients into a cocktail shaker. Shake thoroughly without ice to make the foam. Add ice and shake again until chilled. Strain into a coupe glass. Drink to the certainties of life: death, taxes, and that Mennonite churches will always schism.

The Brethren in Kir

Makes 1 cocktail

It is a truth universally acknowledged that people who live near rivers will eventually want to baptize each other in them. The Brethren in Christ date back to 1780 or so when a bunch of Mennonites and former Mennonites and Lutherans who lived by the Susquehanna River in Pennsylvania grew impassioned about conversion and immersion. Originally called the River Brethren, they've been dipping each other in rivers ever since.

This cocktail immerses blackcurrant liqueur in a flowing river of white wine. The proportions are a bit more in favour of the cassis than the traditional kir recipe. Choose a crisp white wine like a Pinot Gris or a Sauvignon Blanc.

4 oz (125 mL) chilled white wine
½ oz (15 mL) cassis

Pour the wine and cassis directly into a wineglass. Gently stir so that the immersed cassis rises to the top again. Like the souls of the saved. Savour this cocktail on a summer day, especially, but not exclusively, while lingering by the riverside.

Black Russian Soil

Makes 1 cocktail

Some Mennonites have a fondness in our hearts for Catherine the Great of Russia, who invited us to settle in the lands she had recently conquered along the Dnieper River in what is now Ukraine. It's not that she particularly liked Mennonites; she just wanted us there to make it harder for any Ottoman Turks who might have been tempted to try to take the land back again. We Mennonites weren't the only people to answer Catherine's invitation, but we were the only ones who negotiated religious freedom, exemption from military service, control over schooling, and—most importantly—the right to brew beer and distill our own liquors.

The Black Russian cocktail is vodka and a coffee liqueur. This cocktail uses the components of coffee liqueur on their own—because using a store-bought liqueur just isn't in the pioneering spirit.

> 1½ oz (45 mL) vodka
> ½ oz (15 mL) gold rum
> ½ oz (15 mL) cold-brew coffee
> ¼ oz (7.5 mL) vanilla syrup (see page 143)

Pour all ingredients into a mixing glass with ice. Stir together until chilled and well mixed. Strain and serve over ice in an old-fashioned glass, and drink to self-serving despots everywhere who have provided us with homes.

Rum-Springa Cocktail

Makes 1 cocktail

A few short decades before the Age of Enlightenment, the Swiss Brethren in the Alsace region were splitting apart over whether it was okay for their members to share meals with non-members. And also whether it was vain to fasten one's clothes with buttons. In 1693, the schism became final with Jakob Ammann and his followers excommunicating all the lax button-wearers. Later, they apologized for their rashness and excommunicated themselves in contrition. But it was too little too late for the Swiss Brethren (who were now calling themselves Mennonites like the Anabaptists in the Netherlands), and the Amish and the Mennonites have been separate groups ever since.

Today, one thing the Amish are known for is their practice of Rumspringa—a period of adolescent socializing in which some of the rules around technology use are loosened. Mennonites, not being Amish, have nothing so formal. But we can have a cocktail.

> 2 oz (60 mL) dark rum
> 1 oz (30 mL) kirsch
> 4 oz (125 mL) cola

Pour the rum and kirsch directly into an old-fashioned glass with ice. Stir until chilled, and then add the cola and stir gently to mix. Button up your overcoat, and go share this cocktail with a non-Anabaptist neighbour in defiance of Jakob Ammann's memory.

The American Menno

Makes 1 cocktail

Mennonites have been in North America since 1683, and America just wouldn't be the same today if it weren't for us. And I don't just mean that the byways of Pennsylvania would lack the sight of horse and buggies. No, I mean we would be missing important cultural icons that owe their debt to Mennonite founders—like Hershey's chocolate, Smucker's jam, or Old Overholt whiskey.

The Americano is a cocktail created in Italy in a sort of homage to Americans. The American Menno is a twist on the classic, still using Campari as the dominant flavour but adding in a bit of American rye whiskey—use Old Overholt if you can find it.

1 oz (30 mL) Campari
1 oz (30 mL) sweet vermouth
½ oz (15 mL) American rye whisky
Sparkling water to top
An orange twist (see page 147) to garnish

Pour the Campari, vermouth, and rye directly into an old-fashioned glass over ice. Stir until chilled. Add sparkling water, and garnish with an orange twist. Throw the cocktail back, and chase it with a square of chocolate or a spoonful of jam.

The Kirschliche Cocktail

Makes 1 cocktail

In 1860, when the leaders of the Mennonite communities in Russia were still dealing with the social and economic fallout of the Crimean War, a bunch of pious kids stood up and declared that the entire Mennonite community was corrupt beyond repair. The leaders did not take this well, and even had one of the young reformers imprisoned. Still, it might have resolved itself if the newly formed Mennonite Brethren hadn't started derisively calling the established church members "Churchy" (*Kirchliche* in German) Mennonites—an insult that put the disputants outside the path of reconciliation.

This cocktail honours the Mennonite tradition of ambiguous insults and the Mennonite Brethren who proved particularly adept at it. It is a sweet cocktail, and no doubt corrupt beyond repair.

    2 oz (60 mL) dry vermouth
    1 oz (30 mL) kirsch
    1 oz (30 mL) gin
    ½ oz (15 mL) fresh lemon juice
    ¼ oz (7.5 mL) vanilla syrup (see page 143)

Pour all ingredients in a cocktail shaker filled halfway with ice. Shake thoroughly and strain into a coupe glass. Drink this with your friends and community members. In the spirit of reconciliation, even include the churchy ones.

Kleine Gibson

Makes 1 cocktail

The Kleine Gemeinde has the dubious distinction of being the only branch of the faith whose founders actually spoke up against laughter and fun. *Kleine Gemeinde* means "small fellowship"—the movement that started in 1814 stayed small even by Mennonite standards. The Kleine Gemeinde left Ukraine en masse in 1874, and many of their descendants can still be found moping about the Americas.

The Gibson is a serious cocktail for a serious people. Or at least, this one is. This recipe is a traditional Gibson, varying only by insisting on a quick-pickled red rather than a frivolous commercially produced pickled pearl onion.

Several strands of quick-pickled red onion (see page 147)
2 oz (60 mL) gin
1 oz (30 mL) dry vermouth

Place strands of pickled red onion in a coupe or martini glass. Set aside. Put both cocktail ingredients in a mixing glass, and stir with ice until chilled. Strain into the prepared glass. Drink with an appropriate air of solemnity, remembering that Jesus wept in the Bible, but he never laughed.

Vistula Daisy

Makes 1 cocktail

There was a time, back in the mid-1700s in the Vistula delta (that's around the city of Danzig in what is now Poland), when Mennonites grew so famous for their liquors that the terms *Mennonite* and *tavern keeper* were practically synonymous. Sure, that was because the Mennonites who had migrated there from the Netherlands were given limited occupational options by the Prussian government and distilling was one of the few jobs open to them. But I say, when life gives you lemons, make a cocktail.

The Prussian distillers were particularly known for their brandies. If you can get your hands on a Danziger Goldwasser, try substituting that for the brandy—increase it to two ounces (60 mL) and leave out the Chartreuse. This version of a Brandy Daisy uses cognac brandy as it is more readily available.

1½ oz (45 mL) cognac
¾ oz (22 mL) grenadine (see page 145)
½ oz (15 mL) green Chartreuse
½ oz (15 mL) fresh lemon juice
Crushed ice to serve

Pour cognac, grenadine, Chartreuse, and lemon juice into a cocktail shaker filled halfway with ice. Shake thoroughly, and strain into a julep cup or wineglass filled with crushed ice. Serve with a straw while lobbying your local Mennonites to take up the old tradition of tavern keeping.

Johann Cornies Reviver

Makes 1 cocktail

Popularly known at the time as the Mennonite czar, Johann Cornies was an adept administrator who brought innovation, cottage industry, and many, many pretty trees to the little Mennonite villages in the Molotschna Colony in Ukraine. He also brought a spirit of despotism that undermined our basic egalitarian culture, annihilated any sort of free-flowing dialogue, and eroded our traditional opposition to corporal punishment. But the trees are actually really nice.

This cocktail is based on the classic Corpse Reviver No. 2. It adds mulberries in recognition of the many mulberry trees that Cornies ordered planted in a failed attempt to make Mennonites into rich silk producers. If you have no mulberry trees in your vicinity, substitute blackberries or blueberries.

A dash of absinthe
3–4 mulberries, plus more to garnish
1 oz (30 mL) gin
1 oz (30 mL) triple sec
1 oz (30 mL) Lillet Blanc
1 oz (30 mL) fresh lemon juice

Drop the dash of absinthe into a coupe glass, and swirl around to coat the inside of the glass. Set aside. Place mulberries in the bottom of a cocktail shaker. Add the other ingredients. Muddle the mulberries, and then add ice, and shake the cocktail thoroughly until chilled. Strain into the prepared coupe glass, and enjoy the beverage while honouring Cornies's memory by ordering people around about the minutiae of their lives.

The Genever Conference

Makes 1 cocktail

Noteworthy among the leaders of a major North American schism was John H. Oberholtzer, who had stirred up trouble in Pennsylvania in 1847 by having the effrontery to suggest the advisability of a constitution and of maintaining minutes, reforms that the others considered worldly. The new group that came together in 1860 following this dispute became known as the General Conference Mennonite Church. It was allowed to have such an all-encompassing name because the other groups of Mennonites hadn't bothered to draw up a constitution claiming the name for themselves.

This cocktail is not afraid of a little involvement in the world and uses genever, a spirit only known to those Mennonites who are in communication with their Dutch co-religionists.

1 oz (30 mL) genever
¾ oz (22 mL) triple sec
½ oz (15 mL) fresh lemon juice
A dash of aromatic bitters

Pour the genever, triple sec, and lemon juice in a cocktail shaker filled halfway with ice. Shake thoroughly until chilled. Strain into a coupe glass and top with bitters. Drink with friends or community members, taking copious notes in the process.

Old Piña Colony

Makes 1 cocktail

Many Mennonites will say that we like to sing the traditional hymns, but only the Old Colony Mennonites can really lay any claim to that statement. Back in 1880, the group that became known as the Old Colony parted ways with the rest of the Manitoba Mennonites when the latter started singing the hymns written by English, American, and German Christians. The Mennonites soon to be known as the Old Colony Mennonites complained that these new hymns were not traditional and that their catchy melodies and harmonies, furthermore, made them sound like drinking songs. Which was apparently a bad thing.

Old Colony Mennonites are, today, some of the most traditionalist Mennonites in the Americas, with large communities living in relative isolation in Latin America. A piña colada is, likewise, a fairly traditional cocktail.

> **2 oz (60 mL) pineapple juice**
> **2 oz (60 mL) canned coconut milk**
> **½ oz (15 mL) simple syrup (see page 141)**
> **1 oz (30 mL) white rum**

Pour all ingredients into a cocktail shaker filled halfway with ice. Shake thoroughly, and strain into a hurricane or highball glass with ice. Feel free to belt out your favourite hymns while drinking this, in either the old or the new style of singing.

Holdemanhattan

Makes 1 cocktail

John Holdeman fretted at the number of different Christian church sects that all claimed a monopoly on truth. He resolved the problem by establishing yet one more church. "The Church of God in Christ, Mennonite," has been around since 1859, declaring itself the one true church in a world of imposters. Holdeman Mennonites are a plain-dressing group. A stranger might mistake them for members of a Conservative Mennonite congregation. That stranger would be wrong.

The Manhattan is a traditional and fairly plain cocktail that probably gets made more often each day than there are Holdeman Mennonites in the entire world (about 25,000). Since the largest concentration of Holdeman Mennonites is in the US Midwest, try to find a rye whisky that uses prairie grains in their honour.

> 2 oz (60 mL) rye whisky
> 1 oz (30 mL) kirsch
> A dash of aromatic bitters
> A cocktail cherry (see page 147) to garnish

Pour all ingredients except the cherry into a mixing glass, and stir with ice until chilled. Strain into an old-fashioned glass, and serve with ice. Top with a cherry, and drink joyfully, knowing that you are imbibing the one true cocktail.

Paper Plains of North America

Makes 1 cocktail

After Pennsylvania and Ontario had their fill of Mennonites, later migrants went to the American and Canadian prairies. Many of us came from Russia in the 1870s when we didn't like it there anymore. We settled in Manitoba, Nebraska, and Kansas. There were, of course, Indigenous people already living in those lands. We noticed them at first, but after a while, we stopped noticing because we were too distracted by our traditional practice of bickering among ourselves and splitting into more and more smaller groups.

The Paper Plane is a traditional cocktail, though perhaps not as traditional as the habit of Mennonites breaking into schisms. This cocktail uses a simple syrup made from the golden syrup well loved by the Mennonites of the Canadian prairies in lieu of the traditional amaro.

¾ oz (22 mL) bourbon
¾ oz (22 mL) Aperol
¾ oz (22 mL) golden simple syrup (see page 142)
¾ oz (22 mL) fresh lemon juice
A sprig from a saskatoon berry bush to garnish

Pour all ingredients except the garnish into a cocktail shaker filled halfway with ice. Shake and strain into a coupe glass. Garnish with a sprig from a saskatoon berry bush, and sip by the light of the prairie moon. Or at least the thought of one.

Remember the Khanate

Makes 1 cocktail

There's nothing like a good apocalypse to get us up and migrating. Especially if the Second Coming also comes with the promise of better economic opportunities. Historians and also the descendants of the Mennonites who migrated from Russia to Turkestan in 1880 have been arguing ever since as to whether those Mennonites were deluded by talk of the end times or whether they were pragmatic economic emigrants. In any case, those of us who remained in Turkestan ended up being taken in by the khans and living happily ever after as a Mennonite minority among the Muslims, at least until Stalin broke it all up in the 1930s.

Remember the Maine is a cocktail named after an international military insult from around the turn of the 20th century. Remember the Khanate, on the other hand, commemorates a moment of cross-cultural welcome just a little bit earlier.

> 2 oz (60 mL) rye whisky
> ⅓ oz (2 tsp/10 mL) sweet vermouth
> ½ oz (15 mL) kirsch
> A dash of absinthe

Pour all ingredients into a mixing glass. Stir with ice. Strain into a coupe glass, or an old-fashioned glass with ice, and raise your glass with a rallying cry to never ever forget the times when people live in peace and harmony with strangers.

Old Orgeat

Makes 1 cocktail

You know the Old Order Mennonites—they're the ones most people think of when they think about Mennonites. They look a lot like the Amish. It wasn't so much a schism that brought them into being as a whole movement of schisms from the 1870s to the 1900s. This was when various leaders across North America got all hot and bothered about radical innovations that threatened to make us interact more with people outside of the faith. Like women wearing hats and men wearing belts, and everyone putting electricity in their houses. And things like that.

This cocktail is a variation on one called the Black Tie. Old Order Mennonites do not, as a rule, attend black-tie events, and ties are actually forbidden in some groups. Their men do, however, very much favour wearing black pants and jackets.

1½ oz (45 mL) gold rum
½ oz (15 mL) triple sec
¾ oz (22 mL) fresh grapefruit juice
½ oz (15 mL) orgeat (see page 145)
½ oz (15 mL) molasses simple syrup (see page 142)

Pour all ingredients into a cocktail shaker filled halfway with ice. Shake thoroughly, and strain into an old-fashioned glass with ice. Drink this with like-minded folks somewhere far away from the evils of the world.

Conscientious Cobbler

Makes 1 cocktail

Every now and then, world events burst their way into our affairs despite our best efforts to ignore them. For instance, try as we might, we could not miss the two world wars. These were such cataclysmic events that they even got Mennonites of different subsects, who usually never spoke to each other, to come together in an alliance to lobby their governments for exemptions or alternate, non-combatant service assignments. Where we succeeded, our Mennonite young men spent the two world wars working in forestry, hospitals, medical corps, and other non-military service jobs. Where we didn't, they were tarred and feathered.

A cobbler is a mixture of fortified wine and fruit, served over crushed ice like a slushy. It dates back to the 1840s, well before the words *conscientious* and *objector* had come together for those who resisted military service for reasons of faith. This variation uses port and brandy instead of the traditional sherry.

> **A handful of berries or other seasonal fruit**
> **1 oz (30 mL) ruby port**
> **1 oz (30 mL) brandy**
> **1 oz (30 mL) Chambord**
> **¼ oz (7.5 mL) fresh lemon juice (if fruit isn't tart)**
> **Crushed ice to serve**

Place a layer of fruit on the bottom of a cocktail shaker. Add the port, brandy, Chambord, and lemon juice (but omit lemon juice if using tart fruit). Muddle the fruit. Add ice, and shake thoroughly until chilled. Strain into an old-fashioned glass filled with crushed ice. Sip through a straw after a long day's work performing back-breaking non-military service to the world.

Nestor Makhnegroni

Makes 1 cocktail

Mennonites believe in loving our enemies, but we make an exception for Nestor Makhno. Things had been going swimmingly for the Mennonites in Ukraine until the revolution came along in 1917 and decimated our social order, opening us up to war, famine, and pestilence. Nestor Makhno was the Ukrainian anarchist leader who led the charge against the Mennonite villagers. We can't hold him responsible for all our suffering. But we'll try.

The Negroni is a classic cocktail loved around the world by people who love all things bitter. It is every bit as bitter as the most unforgiving Mennonite of the Ukrainian diaspora. One might be tempted to substitute vodka for gin given that Makhno likely drank vodka, not gin. But we're not giving him that.

1 oz (30 mL) Campari
1 oz (30 mL) gin
1 oz (30 mL) sweet vermouth
Several dashes aromatic bitters
An orange twist (see page 147) to garnish

Pour the Campari, gin, and vermouth into a mixing glass, and stir with ice until thoroughly chilled. Strain into an old-fashioned glass over ice. Top with the bitters, and garnish with an orange twist. Imbibe while remembering the Mennonite commonwealth and the man we blame for ruining it all.

The David Martini Mennonites

Honestly. What is the point of having a rule against bicycle riding if you can't even kick people out of the church when you find them cycling around the countryside? In 1917, David Martin grew frustrated with his Old Order Mennonite leaders in Ontario who were refusing to discipline people who rode bicycles. Consequently, he set up his own church (now known as the Independent Old Order Mennonite Church), with a mission to do a better job.

A martini is a blend of gin and dry vermouth. Adding more than the requisite amount of vermouth is not likely to arouse the ire of the David Martin Mennonites (it's just not the sort of thing they care about), but it may raise eyebrows among cocktail purists.

2 oz (60 mL) gin
½ oz (15 mL) dry vermouth
An olive to garnish

Pour all ingredients except the olive into a mixing glass, and stir with ice until chilled. Strain into a martini glass, and add the olive. Enjoy this cocktail at home or with friends, but please remember not to drink and drive (not even a bicycle).

Evana-escent Smashed

Makes 1 cocktail

The schism that is still ongoing in 21st-century North America is perhaps the sexiest of all Mennonite schisms. I mean that literally—it is about sex. For most of our history, Mennonites didn't really talk about sex. But as American evangelicals began concerning themselves with decrying same-sex relationships, we couldn't help overhearing, and pretty soon we were schisming all over the place.

This cocktail's name is derived from the group of churches called the Evana Network, who resurrected two traditions of Mennonite churches that many of us thought were done and over with—being super exclusionary and breaking into schisms. They're not really Mennonites anymore, having fully left the Mennonite Church USA, but this version of a bourbon smash is to help us remember where dogmatism can lead.

½ lemon, in thick slices
3–4 fresh leaves of mint
1 oz (30 mL) simple syrup (see page 141)
2 oz (60 mL) bourbon
3 oz (90 mL) sparkling water
A spring of fresh mint to garnish

Muddle the lemon in the bottom of a cocktail shaker. Add mint, simple syrup, and bourbon, and fill halfway with ice. Shake thoroughly, and strain into a highball glass with ice. Top with sparkling water, and stir gently. Garnish with mint. Raise your glass to a future where Mennonite diversity includes all genders, sexual orientations, and maybe even hymn book preferences. (That last one might be taking things too far.)

MCC Breeze

Makes 1 cocktail

Wherever there are communist parties, there are central committees. The Soviet Union had one, and all of the little communist parties that never took power also had their very own central committees. And we have one too. In 1920, the Mennonites of North America established the Mennonite Central Committee to provide food aid to the Mennonite victims of the Russian Revolution in Ukraine. It is true that the Bolsheviks had their central committee before we had ours, but—so what? Ours is still going, providing food and other types of aid to people all over the world, and theirs deserted the committee room sometime around the fall of the Berlin Wall.

MCC has become core to Mennonite identity over the past hundred years as a rare organization that has buy-in from a wide variety of service-oriented Mennonites. These same Mennonites and more will probably like this variation on the Sea Breeze cocktail.

> 2 oz (60 mL) vodka
> ½ oz (15 mL) unsweetened cranberry juice
> ½ oz (15 mL) fresh grapefruit juice
> ¼ oz (7.5 mL) orgeat (see page 145)

Pour all ingredients into a cocktail shaker filled halfway with ice. Shake thoroughly, and strain into a highball glass with ice. Make several of these for your friends and family and any other people in need.

Chaco Bijou

Makes 1 cocktail

Mennonites have been in Latin America since 1919, and the continent is now veritably swarming with us. In a couple of countries, we even make up 1 percent of the population. Which is about the same as in Canada and way more than in the United States. These tropical Mennonites have now infiltrated all but three of the South American countries and have participated in everything from politics to cheese making. Paraguayan Mennonites number almost 40,000 and have the distinction of having set themselves up in the Chaco, a place they lovingly call the Green Hell.

This cocktail is a variation on the Bijou cocktail. This version features the well-loved South American yerba maté tea that Mennonites there love every bit as much as their neighbours do.

    1 oz (30 mL) yerba maté–infused vodka (see page 146)
    1 oz (30 mL) sweet vermouth
    1 oz (30 mL) elderflower liqueur

Combine all ingredients in a mixing glass, and stir with ice. Strain into a coupe glass, and marvel at the murky jungle-like hues before downing this jewel of a beverage.

Sect of the Beachy

Makes 1 cocktail

The Amish broke from Mennonites back in 1693, but many of the liberal Amish eventually merged back with the Mennonites after a couple of centuries passed and everyone forgot their differences. As a result, most of the Amish who use the term today are Old Order Amish. Except for the Beachy Amish Mennonites, who were Old Order Amish but broke away in 1927 to be a little more Mennonite. And to confuse the hell out of everyone trying to keep track of the distinctions between Amish and Mennonite.

Not only is this cocktail a tribute to Moses Beachy and his fellow Amish Mennonites, it's also a great drink to serve to anyone who really wants a sweet, fruity cocktail but would be too embarrassed to ask for Sex on the Beach.

> 2 oz (60 mL) fresh orange juice
> 2 oz (60 mL) unsweetened cranberry juice
> 1½ oz (45 mL) vodka
> ½ oz (15 mL) peach schnapps
> ½ oz (15 mL) Chambord

Pour all ingredients directly into a highball glass with ice and stir. This cocktail is traditionally garnished with an orange wheel and maraschino cherries, but not to worry, it's okay to question tradition from time to time. But not too much. Garnish as you wish.

Thunderfelder

Makes 1 cocktail

In 1922, about half of the Sommerfeld Mennonites and most of the Old Colony Mennonites had had enough of the Manitoba government reneging on the Canadian government's promise that the Mennonites would have complete control of their schooling. If that happened, they knew that their children would begin speaking English and would, therefore, lose all hope of maintaining their faith. Anticipating that everything would just go from bad to worse in Canada, they packed up their German schoolbooks and left for Mexico.

This cocktail is in honour of the thunderous voices of the Sommerfeld Mennonites objecting to the government's encroachment on their rights and traditions. It is based on a cocktail called the Thunderbird.

1½ oz (45 mL) rye whisky
1 oz (30 mL) amaretto
1 oz (30 mL) pineapple juice
1 oz (30 mL) fresh orange juice
A pineapple wedge to garnish

Pour all ingredients except the garnish into a cocktail shaker filled halfway with ice. Shake thoroughly, and strain into a highball glass with ice. Garnish with a pineapple wedge, and drink while raising your fist (or your suitcase) at government intervention.

New MKC Sour

Makes 1 cocktail

Some of the newest congregations of Mennonites are also the fastest growing. The Mennonites in Ethiopia call themselves the Meserete Kristos Church (MKC). They haven't had any schisms yet, but there's still time. This group started in 1951 and went underground for a number of years, only to start taking off in the 1980s when the political climate improved for Mennonites there. So they lost time that could otherwise have been applied to the important work of petty squabbling that Mennonites elsewhere in the world have perfected over centuries.

The New York sour isn't really a new cocktail, but the Meserete Kristos Mennonites are new Mennonites. This cocktail is similar to the New York sour, but it subs in honey syrup for simple syrup in tribute to the honey wine that is well loved by the people of Ethiopia.

> 2 oz (60 mL) rye whisky
> 1 oz (30 mL) fresh lemon juice
> 1 oz (30 mL) honey simple syrup (see page 141)
> ½ oz (15 mL) hearty red wine

Pour all ingredients except for the red wine into a cocktail shaker filled halfway with ice. Shake thoroughly, and strain into an old-fashioned glass with ice. Float the wine on top by slowly and carefully pouring the wine over the back of a bar spoon onto the top of the iced beverage. Sip in appreciation of all things new.

Now, loyal reader, having worked our way through the history of our beleaguered people and grappled with the issues of doctrine, it is at last time to enjoy some Mennonite culture.

For many of us, being Mennonite is not so much about the religion as it is about the cultural trappings of being part of a group that accidentally became something of an ethnicity after a couple hundred years of avoiding mainstream society. It was accidental in that being a Mennonite is always, by definition, a choice made as an adult. But even those of us who stayed away on Baptism Sundays may lay claim to the things we have come to think of as Mennonite—language, clothing, foods, pastimes, and habits—that sometimes have little to do whatsoever with the doctrines of the church.

This last group of cocktail recipes nods to certain cultural forms that at least some of us have loved and identified as Mennonite for years or decades or even centuries. Do not, however, strain yourself, critical reader, in trying to discern an authentic Mennonite culture in any of these forms. We are many and varied and prone to adapt to our surroundings. But also prone to nostalgia.

We like to think that we were once "The Quiet in the Land," but I suspect it always got louder when you came close enough to hear.

PART IV

QUIET IN THE LIQUOR CABINET

Pennsylvania Cups

Makes 1 cocktail

One of the groups of Mennonites who can claim the title of Mennonite as a heritage are the Mennonites who settled in America from Switzerland and thereabouts and speak a dialect called Pennsylvania Dutch, which isn't Dutch at all and isn't limited to Pennsylvania. Having been in America for a very long time, the descendants of the Pennsylvania Dutch Mennonites are legion, though few of these claim it as an ethnic identity, having forgotten most of their shared history, and only now and then opening up their copies of the *Mennonite Community Cookbook*.

This cocktail is to remind all those Pennsylvania Mennonites and their progeny of their heritage as whisky distillers and chocolate makers.

2 oz (60 mL) rye whisky
½ oz (15 mL) crème de cacao
2 dashes chocolate bitters (optional; see page 148)

Pour all ingredients into a mixing glass, and stir with ice. Strain into an old-fashioned glass and serve as an aperitif, recognizing that this can serve as one of the seven sweets needed for any Pennsylvania Dutch Mennonite meal. Search through your *Mennonite Community Cookbook* for seven sours to accompany it.

Long Explanation Iced Tea

Makes 1 cocktail

It is an irony of history that a people who originally insisted on individual choice in religion developed, in time, into a people who identify as an ethnicity. All this means is that when you meet someone who identifies as Mennonite, you might require a long explanation to understand whether they are a person identifying as a religious, churchgoing Mennonite, a so-called ethnic Mennonite who has not graced the insides of a meeting house in decades, or some combination of the two.

This cocktail is a variation of the Long Island iced tea. But it takes longer.

1 oz (30 mL) gin
1 oz (30 mL) white rum
1 oz (30 mL) tequila
1 oz (30 mL) vodka
1 oz (30 mL) fresh lemon juice
3 oz (90 mL) cola
A lemon wedge and handful of berries to garnish

Fill a highball glass three-quarters full of ice. Add all ingredients except the cola and the garnish. Stir well. Add cola to fill the glass. Garnish with lemon and berries. Drink slowly, questioning the authenticity of each ingredient and each element of a Mennonite identity with every sip.

Pimm's Cape Dress

Makes 1 cocktail

Not all superheroes wear capes, and not all Mennonites wear cape dresses. But some do. Conservative and Old Order Mennonite women wear dresses designed specifically to be plainer than anything that was ever remotely fashionable. The cape dress is distinct from other unfashionable dresses by a square piece of fabric tacked onto the bodice. This does not entirely hide the presence of breasts, but it does as well as can be expected from a small, unassuming piece of cloth. The cape dress is the modest dress that all other modest dresses aspire to, and it is the dress that people who aren't Mennonite think of when they think about Mennonite clothing. When they think about it at all.

The Pimm's Cup cocktail calls for an English liqueur by the same name. This plain version of the Pimm's Cup offers up the same flavour profile in a modest yet fruity summer sipper.

A few strawberries, cucumber slices, and small orange wedges
1 oz (30 mL) orange-infused gin (see page 146)
1 oz (30 mL) sweet vermouth
½ oz (15 mL) fresh lemon juice
½ oz (15 mL) simple syrup (see page 141)
2 oz (60 mL) sparkling water

Fill half of a highball glass with ice, berries, cucumber slices, and orange wedges. Separately combine the orange-infused gin, vermouth, lemon juice, and simple syrup in a mixing glass. Pour over the fruit and ice in the serving glass and top with sparkling water. Enjoy modestly.

Thrift Store Sour

Makes 1 cocktail

We Mennonites have long considered ourselves a frugal people. It wasn't until 1972, however, that Selma Loewen and a few of her friends in Altona, Manitoba, realized that they could monetize the frugality and raise money for overseas mission work. Since that fateful day, Mennonites in various North American communities have channelled all their longings for conspicuous consumption into thrift store bargain hunts while also unloading their debris to the same location.

There is nothing particularly frugal about this version of a pisco sour unless you use bitters that you made a few months back and stored in bottles you found in a thrift store.

1½ oz (45 mL) pisco
1 oz (30 mL) fresh lemon juice
¾ oz (22 mL) vanilla syrup (see page 143)
1 egg white
A few dashes aromatic bitters

Pour all ingredients except for the bitters into a cocktail shaker without ice. Shake thoroughly until the egg white forms a thick foam. Add ice to the shaker, and shake again until the cocktail is chilled. Strain into a coupe glass that you purchased second-hand at a thrift store, top with aromatic bitters, and sip with the satisfaction of knowing that you will also be able to repurpose that pisco bottle into a vase and donate it to the thrift store after you have had just a few more of these.

Plautdietsch Punch

Makes 1 cocktail

They say there is no word for *love* in *Plautdietsch*. Or any other abstract idea for that matter. But it doesn't matter. Plautdietsch, or Low German, was never anyone's only language. Or at least, it hasn't been in a very long time. In some places, Mennonites speak Low German at home, High German in church, and the local language in school or business. Every generation, some of us wring our hands and worry that the language will die with our elders. But, not to worry. It's alive and well and still not talking about love wherever the conservative Old Colony Mennonites are settled.

The Mennonites who speak Plautdietsch (or did until recently) also have a fondness for sorrel, a bitter green herb not unlike spinach that is a core ingredient in our herbaceous *Summa Borscht* soup. This cocktail doesn't taste like the soup at all, but it gets a pleasant sharpness from the sorrel.

> 2 fresh sorrel leaves, plus another to garnish
> ½ oz (15 mL) fresh lime juice
> 2 oz (60 mL) tequila
> 1 oz (30 mL) elderflower liqueur
> 2 oz (60 mL) sparkling water
> Saskatoon berries to garnish

Muddle the sorrel with lime juice in the bottom of a highball glass. Fill the glass with ice. Pour the tequila, elderflower liqueur, and sparkling water over the ice. Stir gently with a bar spoon. Garnish with sorrel and saskatoon berries. It's okay to love this cocktail; just don't imagine you can put that emotion into words.

Blitz Elixir

Makes 1 cocktail

Dutch Blitz is not Dutch, and the *blitz* in the name does not refer to blitzkrieg or anything else that is warlike. It is a fast-paced card game that came out of Pennsylvania, where Mennonites and Amish use the game to teach children colours, numbers, and how to expend violent tendencies without going to war. It involves quickly slamming cards on a table in sequential colour-coded piles. People who have watched Mennonites play Dutch Blitz invariably doubt our pacifism, but it is a fact that no game of Dutch Blitz has ever led to blows among us.

This cocktail is a slammer and requires a shot glass. It is a vonderful goot cocktail and won't take too much time away from the business of playing.

1 oz (30 mL) genever
½ oz (15 mL) rhubarb syrup (see page 144)
½ oz (15 mL) sparkling water

Pour all ingredients directly into a 2 oz (60 mL) shot glass. Cover the glass with the palm of your hand. Lift up and slam back down on the table, with all the ferocity of a Blitz player slamming down the winning card. This will cause the drink to mix and the soda to fizz. Throw the shot back, yell "Blitz!" and set up your cards for the next round.

Duakiri

Makes 1 cocktail

Women in progressive Mennonite communities stopped wearing religious headgear sometime in the mid-20th century. Nowadays, only women in the conservative, separatist branches wear head coverings as an expression of their devotion. Old Order and Conservative Mennonite women wear white mesh head coverings typically held onto their hair with pins. Old Colony Mennonite women wear a black fringed kerchief called a *Düak*. There is no theological reason for this distinction.

The traditional daiquiri is made with rum, sugar, and lime juice, though there are as many variations of the daiquiri as there are variations of head coverings. This one uses rhubarb syrup because rhubarb is well loved by all variations of Mennonites.

2 oz (60 mL) white rum
1 oz (30 mL) fresh lime juice
¾ oz (22 mL) rhubarb syrup (see page 144)
A slice of lime to garnish

Pour the rum, lime juice, and rhubarb syrup into a cocktail shaker filled halfway with ice. Shake thoroughly, and strain into a coupe glass. Garnish with lime. Remember to cover the shaker while preparing the cocktail, but you don't need to cover your head while drinking.

Mennonite Relief Wassail

Makes 1 cocktail

To raise money for missions, Mennonites in many communities in North America get together once a year and throw a "relief sale." We aren't selling relief, except it is the one time a year when Mennonites are allowed to spend money without feeling guilty about it. And that can be a relief. But the real point of the sale is to raise money to send food and blankets and towels and coloured pencils to people in faraway countries who have need of such things. Though no two relief sales are exactly the same, most of them auction off quilts and sell pies and fried food and whatever else takes their fancy. Sometimes there is music (but no dancing) and races (but no prizes). This is the Mennonite idea of fun.

Wassail is traditionally a Christmas holiday beverage, and relief sales traditionally happen in the spring or summer, but as the relief sale is the closest Mennonites get to a festival, let's bring on the festive beverages even in the spring.

4 oz (125 mL) apple cider (non-alcoholic)
1 oz (30 mL) fresh grapefruit juice
½ oz (15 mL) mulling syrup (see page 144)
1½ oz (45 mL) bourbon

Pour the apple cider, grapefruit juice, and mulling syrup into a pot, and heat until almost boiling. Pour into a serving cup (a teacup or small mug is best), and add the bourbon. Hold the beverage high in front of you, and auction it off to the highest bidder. Give that money to charity, and make another for yourself.

Aperol Quilts

Makes 1 cocktail

Mennonites did not invent quilting and rarely even design our own quilt patterns. But that doesn't prevent us from claiming quilts as one of our cultural forms of expression. We like to think that quilts reflect our values of practicality, frugality, and community. They reflect practicality because they are things of beauty but also useful; frugality, because they are made from fabric scraps or old shirts; and community, because they are made by groups at quilting bees. None of those things are consistently true, but quilts do reflect our value of underpaying women for back-breaking labour.

This cocktail is like if you took an Aperol spritz, cut it up into little pieces, and then sewed it back together again. Sort of.

2 oz (60 mL) Aperol
½ oz (15 mL) fresh lemon juice
½ oz (15 mL) simple syrup (see page 141)
2 oz (60 mL) chilled sparkling wine

Pour the Aperol, lemon juice, and simple syrup directly into a wineglass, and stir to combine. Add ice and sparkling wine. Stir gently, and imbibe while taking a break from cutting and sewing together tiny pieces of fabric for little compensation.

Singalong Sling

Makes 1 cocktail

Mennonites do not limit our singing to the church sanctuary and have been known to break out in song in parks, airplanes, and other public places where our harmonizing might rightly be considered a nuisance. We might be more greatly appreciated if we broadened our repertoire to include songs popular among the wider music-listening public. But no. We are still just singing hymns.

This variation of a Singapore sling promises to be significantly more popular than Mennonite singalongs. At least among people outside our faith community.

> **2 oz (60 mL) pineapple juice**
> **½ oz (15 mL) fresh lime juice**
> **½ oz (15 mL) grenadine (see page 145)**
> **1½ oz (45 mL) gin**
> **¼ oz (7.5 mL) triple sec**
> **¼ oz (7.5 mL) kirsch**
> **¼ oz (7.5 mL) green Chartreuse**
> **A cocktail cherry (see page 147) and pineapple wedge to garnish**

Pour all ingredients except the garnish into a cocktail shaker filled halfway with ice. Shake vigorously, and strain into a highball glass filled with ice. Garnish with a cherry and a pineapple wedge. Down this cocktail in between the first and third verses of your favourite hymn, letting it tickle your tonsils and keep those vocal cords warmed (it's always all right to skip the second verse).

Knacksot and Tonic

It is a rare snack food that doubles as a floor polish. The sunflower seed, however, is one such versatile morsel. Though we know that Mennonites began cultivating and snacking on sunflower seeds sometime in the 19th century, we don't know exactly when our ancestors discovered that spitting the shells onto the wooden floors of their houses oiled the wood and gave the floors a pleasant shine. Not a lot of Mennonites will admit today to continuing this tradition, though there is still plenty of love, especially among the Manitoba and some Latin American Mennonites, for *Knack*-ing *sot* (that's Low German for cracking the shells between your teeth and simultaneously eating the seeds while spitting out the husks).

Several crafters of cocktails have produced libations that honour the sunflower, but these tend to reference the big yellow flower itself, and ignore the little seeds that we love so much. Like the other sunflower cocktails, this one features elderflower liqueur for the floral bouquet. In other ways, it is much like a gin and tonic.

2 oz (60 mL) gin
1 oz (30 mL) elderflower liqueur
Tonic water to top
An orange wedge to garnish
1 bag of roasted sunflower seeds

Pour the gin and elderflower liqueur directly into an old-fashioned glass. Add ice. Top with tonic water and stir. Gently squeeze a bit of orange juice from the wedge into the beverage, and then use the wedge as a garnish. Grab a handful of sunflower seeds, and alternate knacking sot with sipping, being careful that only the shells end up on the floor.

The Sazerook

Makes 1 cocktail

There was a time when some Mennonite groups saw card games in general as inappropriately worldly and banned them from the list of acceptable social activities. But the card game Rook was exempted based on the cards not displaying worldly symbols like kings and queens. The only questionable card is the Rook card, which features an image of a big black bird. But we've all decided it has no symbolic significance whatsoever and so play Rook with abandon. It is a trick-taking game like whist, with as many variations to the rules as there are sects of Mennonites.

Variations to the Sazerac are as subtle as the distinctions between Mennonite groups. It is a classic cocktail recipe demanding a hint of absinthe and Peychaud's bitters mixed with either brandy or rye whisky—which is perfect because Prussian Mennonites were once known as brandy makers and American Mennonites distilled rye. While I encourage you to make your own bitters (and I have found that star anise and cardamom bitters are a pleasant combination), purists would say to stick with Peychaud's.

A dash of absinthe
¼ oz (7.5 mL) simple syrup (see page 141)
2 dashes Peychaud's bitters (or 1 dash each of star anise and cardamom bitters; see page 148)
2 oz (60 mL) rye whisky (or cognac)
A lemon twist (see page 147) to garnish

Pour the absinthe into an old-fashioned glass, and swish it around so that it coats the glass. Set aside. In a mixing glass, combine the simple syrup and the bitters and then add the whisky (or cognac). Stir with ice until thoroughly chilled. Strain into the prepared old-fashioned glass. Squeeze the lemon oils from the twist into the cocktail, and then toss the twist in, and enjoy with all the swagger of a Mennonite college student holding the Rook card.

Crokimule

Makes 1 cocktail

Nothing sounds like fun to the Mennonites of Canada quite so much as a crokinole tournament. First invented by Ontario non-Mennonites in the 1860s, the game consists of little more than flicking checkers across a smooth round wooden board. It quickly grew popular among Mennonites both in Ontario and in the West. The game is a rare recreational activity that finds favour among both the branches of the faith that spurn intellectual activity as worldly and the branches that dislike ornamentation as evidence of vanity. Even progressive Mennonites have been known to take time away from their social justice causes for a game or two of *Kjnipsbrat*.

A simple game like crokinole demands a simple cocktail like a mule. A mule is a cocktail that mixes ginger beer with a spirit—the most famous being the Moscow mule that consists of ginger beer and vodka. This mule calls for Canadian rye whisky because few Mennonites and non-Mennonites outside of Canada have ever tested their index fingers on the crokinole board.

2 oz (60 mL) Canadian rye whisky
½ oz (15 mL) fresh lime juice
5 oz (150 mL) ginger beer
A slice of lime to garnish

Pour the rye and lime juice directly into a Moscow mule mug or highball glass filled with ice. Top with ginger beer, and garnish with lime. Slide the finished cocktail across the table to your opponent, scoring points if you hit another glass along the way. Make another for yourself.

Faspa

There is a ritual called *Faspa* that is sacred to Russian Mennonites and bizarrely anticlimactic to all other Mennonites and non-Mennonites alike. To the naysayers, faspa is nothing more than a cold lunch served midafternoon or whenever. They have a point. None of us, in fact, can agree upon the essential elements that distinguish a faspa from any other cold lunch. Nonetheless, it is one of those things that we know when we see. And we are invariably overjoyed to see it and delighted to be invited to partake.

Martini variations are as ubiquitous as cold lunches. The Faspa cocktail is a variation on the Vesper cocktail, which is itself a variation on the vodka martini.

> **2 oz (60 mL) vodka**
> **1½ oz (45 mL) Lillet Blanc**
> **¾ oz (22 mL) pear brandy**
> **A long lemon twist (see page 147) to garnish**

Pour all ingredients except the garnish into a cocktail shaker filled halfway with ice. Shake vigorously, and strain into a coupe glass. Garnish with lemon twist, and serve in the late afternoon with bread and cheese and jam to whoever happens to be dropping by.

PlumeMimosa

Of all the foods that the Russian Mennonites call their own after having appropriated and adapted cultural foods of the people around us, *Plumemooss* may be the most loved and hated. Done wrong, it is a soupy mess of old fruit. Done right, it is still a soupy mess of old fruit, but it is sublime. Some of us contend that the difference between subpar and sublime is the inclusion of the all-important damson plum that turns the mooss a glorious purple, richer in colour than any robe placed on a wise man in a Christmas pageant and far better in flavour.

A mimosa is typically a brunch cocktail combining orange juice and sparkling wine. The PlumeMimosa is a bit stronger than that, just in case you need to fight off some plumemooss haters at your family brunch gatherings. It replaces the orange juice with damson plum–infused vodka and simple syrup.

1 oz (30 mL) damson plum–infused vodka (see page 146)
¼ oz (7.5 mL) simple syrup (see page 141)
2 oz (60 mL) chilled sparkling wine

Pour infused vodka directly into the bottom of a champagne flute or coupe glass. Mix in the simple syrup. Top with sparkling wine, and gently stir to combine. Say a toast to the almighty damson plum and the Mennonites who learned to include it in their mooss.

The Last Wurst

Makes 1 cocktail

I know vegetarian Mennonites who make an exception for Mennonite farmer's sausage. Back in the olden days in Russia, the whole village would get together for a pig-butchering party and then divvy up the meat for sausage, which they smoked by hanging it in their living-room chimneys. After the butchering, they'd hang around and drink. Some of these old traditions have been lost—Mennonite farmer's sausage that's on the market today still has a unique tanginess, but it's not from being hung through the winter in our personal fireplaces. Goodbye to that tradition, but hello to reviving the drinking part.

Based on the classic The Last Word, this cocktail cuts back on the lime and adds a few dashes of bitters. For digestion.

1 oz (30 mL) gin
1 oz (30 mL) green Chartreuse
1 oz (30 mL) maraschino liqueur
½ oz (15 mL) fresh lime juice
3 dashes aromatic bitters
A lime wedge or cocktail cherries (see page 147) to garnish

Pour all ingredients except the garnish into a cocktail shaker filled halfway with ice. Shake vigorously, and strain into a coupe glass. Garnish with lime or cherries. Serve with sausage.

More-with-Lillet

As long as we have been claiming foods as our own, we have been writing recipes down in Mennonite cookbooks. This tradition took an unexpected turn in 1976, however, when Doris Janzen Longacre came along and wrote the *More-with-Less Cookbook*, which included not only recipes but also a 50-page exhortation in the preface, chastising us for overspending, overeating, and preferring cakes and pies over lentils. This combination sermon and cookbook quickly became the wedding gift favourite for a whole generation of Mennonites and is responsible for all of the underspiced legume-based casseroles that have graced Mennonite potluck tables ever since.

The *More-with-Less Cookbook* does not have a cocktail section, and this cocktail is unlikely to have appeared there if it did have one. If you really want to be frugal, just put some Lillet Blanc on ice and be done with it.

> 2 oz (60 mL) Lillet Blanc
> ½ oz (15 mL) brandy
> ½ oz (15 mL) triple sec
> ¼ oz (7.5 mL) fresh lemon juice
> 1 egg white (optional)
> A thin slice of orange to garnish

Pour all ingredients except the garnish into a cocktail shaker. If using egg white, shake thoroughly without ice until frothy, lifting the lid occasionally to allow air to escape. (Skip this step if not using egg white.) Add some ice and shake until chilled. Pour into a coupe glass, and top with a thin slice of orange. Serve with lentils.

Shoofly Rye

Makes 1 cocktail

Legend has it that the shoofly pie acquired its name because the Pennsylvania Dutch Mennonites, being pacifists, refused to kill the flies that landed on their sugar pies and just politely shooed them away. It's not an authentic legend, but the shoofly pie is an authentic dessert of the Pennsylvania Dutch Mennonites. It is so authentic that there are two versions of it—the dry bottom and the wet bottom—and devotees of each variant. So far, the two groups have managed to live in peace with their differences, but there are rumours of a schism.

All shoofly pies contain a strong dose of molasses, and some have cinnamon. This cocktail has both.

> **2 oz (60 mL) rye whisky**
> **¼ oz (7.5 mL) molasses simple syrup (see page 142)**
> **A dash of cinnamon liqueur**

Pour all ingredients into a mixing glass, and stir with ice until chilled. Serve in an old-fashioned glass over more ice, and keep clear of the houseflies.

Daut Oolt Plauts

Makes 1 cocktail

Plauts is a Russian Mennonite dessert. Though technically the word just means "square," to us it means a cakey bottom covered with a thin layer of fruit and then topped with crumbs and baked. Beyond that, the recipe is open to reinvention, and nobody seems to mind. Mess with our bread recipes or *Varenikje* at your peril, but do what you like with plauts. Go ahead and use a short crust or something more like a butter cake; you can even make it with a bread crust, or pastry. It doesn't matter. And we won't even argue if it is better made with cherries or peaches or plums or apples. It's almost as if we, as a people, can be open to diversity. In dessert, anyway.

The Vieux Carré is a classic cocktail with a name that means "old square." *Daut oolt Plauts* is Plautdietsch for "old square," but in this case it refers to a day-old piece of cake. Which is fine. You can eat it the second day if you like. I suggest not waiting a day, however, to drink the cocktail.

A dash of absinthe
¾ oz (22 mL) rye whisky
¾ oz (22 mL) cognac
¾ oz (22 mL) sweet vermouth
¼ oz (7.5 mL) Chartreuse
A dash of Angostura bitters
A lemon twist (see page 147) to garnish

Drop a dash of absinthe into an old-fashioned glass, and swirl around to coat the inside of the glass. Set aside. Pour all other ingredients except the garnish into a mixing glass, and stir with ice until chilled. Add ice to the prepared glass, and strain mixed cocktail over the ice. Serve with a twist of lemon and a piece of plauts on the side. It doesn't matter what kind. Honest.

LARGE-QUANTITY COCKTAILS

If Mennonites of your acquaintance know that you have this book and that you have developed even a modicum of skill in the preparation of beverages, it is only a matter of time before you will be called upon to provide the beverages at a potluck, congregational retreat, barn raising, quilting bee, or any other such large group gathering. While you could, in theory, shake and stir individual cocktails for all attendees, that is both time consuming and tiring. Instead, I suggest concocting the sort of cocktail that works well for a crowd—one that can be made and served by the pitcher or punch bowl, and that is light enough that none of the event's attendees will embarrass themselves by misquoting Menno Simons, singing off-key, or playing a sloppy game of Dutch Blitz.

The following recipes can easily be made in pitchers and stirred in quantity rather than stirred or shaken individually. Multiply the quantities by the number of servings you desire. (If needed, refer to the conversion chart at the back of the book; e.g., 10 ounces = 1¼ cups.) Stir ingredients (except for anything carbonated) in a pitcher or punch bowl with ice, and if the recipe calls for it, top with the carbonated liquid. Pour your own cocktail first, and then settle for standing at the far end of the potluck line, making the best of the maxim that the first shall be last.

Poly-Gin-and-Juice (page 16)
Pilgram Marpunch (page 27)
Bloody Martyr (page 31)
Dirk 'n' Willemsy (page 35)

Should you ever be asked to provide cocktails to a barn raising or an event with the equivalent expected attendance, you might want to be prepared for the quantities involved in your commitment. For example, for a barn raising, you would need about 500 servings of something like the Pilgram Marpunch. The recipe for such a quantity is as follows:

Twenty 24 oz (750 mL) bottles gold rum

Five 24 oz (750 mL) bottles triple sec

7.5 quarts (7.5 L) apple cider

30 cups (7.5 L) English breakfast tea, brewed and chilled
    (about 10 pots of tea/10 tea bags)

Apple slices

Mix ingredients in a large watering trough or cleaned-out rain barrel with ice and apple slices. Serve over ice, limiting the work crew to one cocktail per person.

SYRUPS AND OTHER PRESERVES

Syrups

Many cocktails use simple syrup as a sweetener, and it is the base for many of the flavoured syrups in the cocktails in this book. As Mennonites can be a bit touchy about being called "simple," feel free to call this "plain syrup" when among your more sensitive Mennonite acquaintances. In truth, though, this syrup is very simple to make. Some syrups are available commercially—orgeat and grenadine being the most common—but I have included recipes just so you can feel guilty about using store-bought.

Simple Syrup
Makes about ½ cup (125 mL)
> ½ cup (125 mL) white sugar
> ½ cup (125 mL) water

Heat the sugar and water in a small pot to boiling, stirring until sugar is dissolved. Cool. Syrup keeps in the fridge for 2–3 weeks.

Honey Simple Syrup
Makes about ½ cup (125 mL)
> ¾ cup (185 mL) honey
> ¼ cup (60 mL) water

Heat the honey and water in a small pot to boiling, stirring until honey is dissolved. Cool. Syrup keeps in the fridge for 2–3 weeks.

Golden Simple Syrup
Makes about ½ cup (125 mL)

½ cup (125 mL) golden syrup
½ cup (125 mL) water

Heat the syrup and water in a small pot to boiling, stirring until dissolved. Cool. Syrup keeps in the fridge for 2–3 weeks. If you cannot find golden syrup in your grocery stores, you can make your own:

Golden Syrup
Makes about 1 cup (250 mL)

2 cups (500 mL) white sugar
½ cup (125 mL) water
1½ Tbsp (22.5 mL) fresh lemon juice

Heat the sugar and water in a pot to boiling, stirring only at the beginning to dissolve. Add the lemon juice and reduce heat to low. Do not stir but rather swirl the pot from time to time to ensure even cooking. Simmer on very low heat for about an hour until it turns a deep amber colour. Remove from heat. Cool slightly before transferring to a glass storage jar. The syrup keeps at room temperature for 6–8 weeks.

Molasses Simple Syrup
Makes about ½ cup (125 mL)

2 Tbsp (30 mL) molasses
¼ cup (60 mL) packed brown sugar
½ cup (125 mL) water

Heat the molasses, sugar, and water in a small pot to boiling, stirring until sugar is dissolved. Cool. Syrup keeps in the fridge for 2–3 weeks.

Brown Sugar Syrup
Makes about ½ cup (125 mL)

¼ cup (60 mL) white sugar
¼ cup (60 mL) packed brown sugar
½ cup (125 mL) water

Heat the sugars and water in a small pot to boiling, stirring until sugar is dissolved. Cool. Syrup keeps in the fridge for 2–3 weeks.

Mint Brown Sugar Syrup

Makes about ½ cup (125 mL)

> ¼ cup (60 mL) fresh mint leaves
> ¼ cup (60 mL) white sugar
> ¼ cup (60 mL) packed brown sugar
> ½ cup (125 mL) water

Heat the mint, sugars, and water in a small pot to boiling, stirring until sugar is dissolved. Cool. Syrup keeps in the fridge for 2–3 weeks.

Vanilla Syrup

Makes about ½ cup (125 mL)

> ½ cup (125 mL) white sugar
> ½ cup (125 mL) water
> About 1-inch (2 cm) piece vanilla bean, sliced open lengthwise

Heat the sugar, water, and vanilla bean in a small pot to boiling, stirring until sugar is dissolved. Cool. Syrup keeps in the fridge for 2–3 weeks.

Ginger Syrup

Makes about ½ cup (125 mL)

> ½ cup (125 mL) white sugar
> ½ cup (125 mL) water
> About 1-inch (2 cm) piece fresh ginger, unpeeled and kept whole

Heat the sugar, water, and ginger in a small pot to boiling, stirring until sugar is dissolved. Cool. Syrup keeps in the fridge for 2–3 weeks.

Star Anise Syrup

Makes about ½ cup (125 mL)

> ½ cup (125 mL) white sugar
> ½ cup (125 mL) water
> 2–3 pods of star anise

Heat the sugar, water, and star anise in a small pot to boiling, stirring until sugar is dissolved. Cool. Syrup keeps in the fridge for 2–3 weeks.

Mulling Syrup

Makes about ¾ cup (185 mL)

>1 cup (250 mL) white sugar
>½ cup (125 mL) water
>¼ cup (60 mL) maple syrup
>4 tsp (20 mL) ground nutmeg
>½ Tbsp (7.5 mL) whole cloves
>4 cinnamon sticks

Put all ingredients in a pot, and heat over medium-high heat until boiling. Boil about 5 minutes, and then remove from the heat. Cool. Syrup keeps in the fridge for 2–3 weeks.

Rhubarb Syrup

Makes about ½ cup (125 mL)

>3 cups (750 mL) chopped rhubarb
>½ cup (125 mL) white sugar
>½ cup (125 mL) water

Heat the rhubarb, sugar, and water in a small pot to boiling, stirring until sugar is dissolved. Cool. Syrup keeps in the fridge for 2–3 weeks.

Strawberry-Rhubarb Syrup

Makes about ½ cup (125 mL)

>1 cup (250 mL) coarsely chopped rhubarb
>1 cup (250 mL) sliced strawberries
>1 tsp (5 mL) fresh lemon juice
>2 Tbsp (30 mL) white sugar
>Enough boiling water to cover

Mix rhubarb, strawberries, lemon juice, and sugar in a bowl or large Mason jar. Cover with boiling water. Let sit for several hours or overnight. Purée in a blender, and strain through a fine-mesh sieve. Syrup keeps in the fridge for 2–3 weeks.

Orgeat

Makes about ½ cup (125 mL)

> ¾ cup (185 mL) white sugar
> ½ cup plus 2 Tbsp (155 mL) water
> ¾ cup (185 mL) almond meal
> **A drop or two of orange flower water or rosewater**

Heat the sugar and water in a pot to boiling, stirring until dissolved. Add the almonds, cook on low heat for 3–4 minutes, and then raise heat until almost boiling. Remove from the heat and cover. Let sit for 3–8 hours. Strain through cheesecloth or a fine-mesh sieve, reserving the almonds for baking or eating. Add orange flower water or rosewater. Syrup keeps in the fridge for 2–3 weeks. This has a stronger almond flavour than the commercially available orgeat; you may wish to reduce the quantity or dilute with water in cocktails.

Grenadine

Makes about ½ cup (125 mL)

> ½ cup (125 mL) white sugar
> ½ cup (125 mL) pomegranate juice
> **One 1-inch (2 cm) strip of orange peel**

Heat the sugar, juice, and orange peel in a small pot until boiling, stirring until sugar is dissolved. Reduce heat. Cover and simmer for 10–15 minutes. Remove orange peel. Cool. Syrup keeps in the fridge for 2–3 weeks.

Infusions

Orange-Infused Gin
Makes about 1 cup (250 mL)

> **1 orange**
> **About 1 cup (250 mL) gin**

Chop the orange into wedges, leaving peel on. Place in a glass jar and top with the gin. Let sit 6 hours or longer. Strain through a sieve.

Damson Plum–Infused Vodka
Makes about 1 cup (250 mL)

> **1 cup (250 mL) damson plums, kept whole and unpeeled**
> **1 cup (250 mL) vodka**

Place the plums in a glass jar, and top with the vodka. Let sit for 6 hours or longer. Strain through a sieve.

Yerba Maté–Infused Vodka
Makes about ¾ cup (185 mL)

> **½ cup (125 mL) yerba maté loose tea**
> **1 cup (250 mL) vodka**

Place yerba maté in a glass jar, and top with vodka. Let sit for 3 hours or longer. Strain through a fine-mesh sieve or cheesecloth.

Garnishes

Lemon Twist

Makes 1 twist

Follow the same method for orange, lime, or grapefruit twists.

1 lemon

For a short lemon twist, use a zester or paring knife to cut a small strip of peel from the lemon, leaving the white pith behind. Twist with your fingers before using as a garnish on the edge of the cocktail glass. For a longer twist, cut a thin slice of the lemon at the widest girth. Cut through the slice and separate the peel from the white pith and inner fruit. Wind the peel into a spiral, and place a weight on it until you are ready to use it as a garnish.

Quick-Pickled Red Onions

Makes about 1 cup (250 mL)

½ red onion, thinly sliced

½ cup (125 mL) white vinegar

A pinch of white sugar

A pinch of salt

Combine all ingredients, and let sit, covered, for an hour or longer.

Boozy Maraschino Cherries

Makes 2 cups (500 mL)

1 pint (2 cups/500 mL) fresh sour cherries, pitted

1 cup (250 mL) maraschino liqueur

Pack cherries into a glass jar, and cover with the maraschino liqueur. Let sit for at least a week.

Bitters

Many of the recipes in this book ask for a dash or two of aromatic bitters. Should you wish
to make your own, note that it will take several months before you can use them. The recipes
require a high-proof grain alcohol. These recipes use 94% alcohol. If using 75%, adjust the dilution
accordingly. Any of the recipes that call for aromatic bitters can be made with rhubarb bitters,
chokecherry bitters, or plain angelica bitters. A few recipes suggest chocolate, star anise, or
cardamom bitters. The recipes below are plainer than any that can be found commercially, but
if you are feeling fancy, you can add other spices and flavouring agents. Each recipe makes about
a cup of bitters, which will last a very long time since they are used by the drop or dash. Perhaps
you can convince the members of your sewing circle or Bible study group to each make a different
kind, and then you can share the products as an act of mutual aid.

Plain Bitters (Rhubarb or Chokecherry)
Makes about 1 cup (250 mL)

> ⅓ cup (80 mL) finely chopped rhubarb or whole chokecherries
> ½ cup (125 mL) high-proof grain alcohol
> 1 cup (250 mL) water
> 1 Tbsp (15 mL) white sugar

Place the rhubarb or chokecherries (the bittering agent) in the bottom of a Mason jar,
and cover with the grain alcohol. Let sit, shaking daily for 15 days. Strain the infused
alcohol, reserving both the solids and liquid. Put the solids in a pot with the water and
sugar. Muddle and then bring to a boil. Simmer for 5–10 minutes. Transfer to a clean
Mason jar, and let sit for 5–7 days, shaking daily. Strain the water infusion. Combine
equal amounts of the reserved infused alcohol and infused water, and decant into small
bottles. Let sit for at least a month before using. Bitters keep unrefrigerated for several
years.

Slightly Fancier Bitters
(Plain Angelica, Chocolate, Star Anise, or Cardamom)
Makes about 1 cup (250 mL)

> 1 tsp (5 mL) dried angelica root
> 1 whole nutmeg and 1-inch (2 cm) piece of cinnamon stick OR 1 tsp (5 mL) cacao nibs OR 2 pods of star anise OR 3 green cardamom pods (flavouring agent; optional)
> ½ cup (125 mL) high-proof grain alcohol
> 1 cup (250 mL) water
> 1 Tbsp (15 mL) white sugar

Place the angelica root and the flavouring agent, if using, in the bottom of a Mason jar, and cover with the grain alcohol. Let sit, shaking daily for 15 days. Strain the infused alcohol, reserving both the solids and liquid. Put the solids in a pot with the water and sugar. Muddle and then bring to a boil. Simmer for 5–10 minutes. Transfer to a clean Mason jar, and let sit for 5–7 days, shaking daily. Strain the water infusion. Combine equal amounts of the reserved infused alcohol and infused water, and decant into small bottles. Let sit for at least a month before using. Bitters keep unrefrigerated for several years.

SUNDAY SCHOOL SIPPERS

Many of the cocktails can be converted into non-alcoholic beverages that will please both the children in your congregation and the adults who prefer to avoid alcohol for reasons of religion, health, or preference, because they have to drive after the event, or because in a moment of desperate frugality, they claimed teetotaller status for the sake of lower insurance premiums and are now bound to their word.

Some of the cocktails in this book do not convert easily into non-alcoholic beverages, and abstemious readers will need to enjoy these only by proxy. The following are instructions for converting the more adaptable cocktails into beverages suitable for morning as well as evening devotions.

Alive in the Age of Reform. Substitute star anise syrup (page 143) for the Pernod and sparkling water for the sparkling wine in the Death in the Age of Reform. **page 15**

Poly-No-Gin-and-Juice. Omit the gin in the Poly-Gin-and-Juice. **page 16**

Brandyless Anabaptist. Omit the brandy in the Brandy Anabaptist. **page 17**

Conrad Grebellini Lite. Substitute ginger ale for the sparkling wine in the Conrad Grebellini. **page 18**

Margret Hottingwallflower. Omit the vodka, and substitute orgeat (page 145) for the amaretto in the Margret Hottingwallbanger. **page 19**

Pilgram Mar-peck on the Cheek. Omit the rum and substitute fresh orange juice for the triple sec in the Pilgram Marpunch. **page 27**

Stras-free-of-bourbon. Omit the bourbon, and substitute fresh orange juice for the triple sec in the Strasbourbon. **page 30**

Bloody Virgin Martyr. Omit the vodka in the Bloody Martyr. **page 31**

Maeyken's Milkshake. Omit the rum, and substitute pear juice for the pear liqueur in the Maeyken's Boozy Milkshake. **page 33**

Dirk 'n' Willemsy's Chaser. Omit the rum in the Dirk 'n' Willemsy. **page 35**

The Baroness von Freeberg. Omit the gin in the Baroness von Freyberg. **page 36**

Upon Exploration of Fizz. Omit the gin in the Upon Confession of Fizz. **page 42**

Youthful Baptiki. Omit the rum and triple sec and increase the quantity of orange juice in the Mode of Baptiki. **page 43**

Peachwater Tea. Omit the Campari and substitute peach juice for the peach schnapps in the CPT: Crimson Peachwater Tea. **page 45**

True Frangelico Faithlessness. Substitute a teaspoon (5 mL) of nutella for the Frangelico in the True Frangelico Faith. **page 48**

Mulled Weakness. Substitute apple cider for the wine in the Mulled Witness. **page 49**

Mutual (Lemon) Words of Assurance. Omit the vodka and substitute green tea for the Chartreuse in the Mutual (Lemon) Aid. **page 53**

Non-alco-nonconformopolitan. Omit the vodka and substitute fresh orange juice for the triple sec in the Nonconformopolitan. **page 55**

Really Plain Plainoma. Omit the tequila in the Plainoma. **page 57**

Not-That-Fancy Navel. Substitute peach juice for the peach schnapps, raspberry juice for the Chambord, and ginger ale for the sparkling wine in the Fancy Navel. **page 59**

(French) 75-Minute Temperance-Themed Service. Omit the gin and brown sugar syrup and substitute ginger ale for the sparkling wine in the (French) 75-Minute Service. **page 63**

Four-Part Singing Sober. Omit the triple sec and kirsch and substitute fruit juice for the wine in the Four-Part Sangria. **page 65**

Migrate without Rita. Omit the tequila and substitute fresh orange juice for the triple sec in the Migratarita. **page 71**

The Brethren sans Kir. Substitute blackberry syrup for the cassis and sparkling water for the white wine in the Brethren in Kir. **page 74**

Fallow Russian Soil. Omit the rum and vodka in the Black Russian Soil. **page 75**

The Kirschless Cocktail. Omit the gin and substitute cherry juice for the kirsch and white grape juice for the vermouth in the Kirschliche Cocktail. **page 80**

Old and Toothless Piña Colony. Omit the rum in the Old Piña Colony. **page 87**

MC Gentle C Breeze. Omit the vodka in the MCC Breeze. **page 100**

Modest Sect of the Beachy. Omit the vodka and substitute peach juice for the peach schnapps and raspberry juice for the Chambord in the Sect of the Beachy. **page 103**

Thunderfreeder. Omit the whisky and substitute orgeat for the amaretto in the Thunderfelder. **page 105**

Pimmsless Cape Dress. Substitute fresh orange juice for the gin and grape juice for the vermouth in the Pimm's Cape Dress. **page 113**

Plautdietsch Nudge. Omit the tequila and substitute elderflower cordial for the elderflower liqueur in the Plautdietsch Punch. **page 117**

Mennonite Relief Wasn't Assail. Omit the bourbon in the Mennonite Relief Wassail. **page 121**

Spiritless Singalong Sling. Omit the gin and substitute green tea for the Chartreuse, orange juice for the triple sec, and cherry juice for the kirsch in the Singalong Sling. **page 124**

Not Sot and Tonic. Omit the gin and substitute elderflower cordial for the elderflower liqueur in the Knacksot and Tonic. **page 125**

PlumeMimo-sans Alcohol. Substitute a small spoonful of damson plum jam for the infused vodka and ginger ale for the sparkling wine in the PlumeMimosa. **page 131**

The Less Wurst. Omit the gin and substitute green tea for the Chartreuse and cherry juice for the maraschino liqueur in the Last Wurst. **page 133**

Acknowledgements

I close this book with a grateful heart for all who led me in the ways of the Mennonite and the ways of the mixologist. Both my family members and my church family versed me in the ways of our people, but it was only after I had left for some time and wandered in the worldlier parts of North America that I came to see the humour of it all. And so I thank both my Mennonite mentors and those friends and acquaintances of mine who never heard the word *Mennonite* until they crossed my path.

Particular thanks go to my family—my father's family, who kept me informed of the culture of Plautdietsch and the Manitoba Mennonites, and my mother's family, who embraced the *Russländer* spirit and offered me tips on infusing damson plums in vodka. I am also fortunate that my parents chose to raise me in Kitchener–Waterloo, where I had the opportunity to absorb some of the culture of Pennsylvania Dutch Mennonites who lived there before us. My mother passed away before I could complete this project, but her support was always important to me, especially because she failed to see the humour in so many of the stories that make up this book. My father passed away even earlier, but his siblings and some of his friends assure me that he would have smiled and laughed quietly to himself had he had the opportunity to read this book. And then he would have disputed my interpretation of the history.

People who offered useful comments, encouragement, and advice and/or helped test cocktail recipes include Svinda Heinrichs, Marilyn Zehr, Marlene Epp, Magdalene Redekop, Alexandra Marin, Clayton Childress, Heather Finley, Alison Li, Charles Hayter, Marianne Fedunkiw, Michelle Harvey, Kimberly de Witte, Anne-Marie Heinrichs, John Bannon, Kate Lewis, Tilman Lewis, Andrea Loewen, Renee Martens, Glen Jones, Pamela Klassen, John Marshall, Rebecca Janzen, Natalie Goosen, Heather Raines, Angela Hamilton, and Beth Dhuey.

Special thanks to Taryn Boyd and the whole team at TouchWood Editions for seeing the potential in this project, to Grace Yaginuma for her meticulous editing, and Mike Hepher for all the fun illustrations. It's been such a pleasure working with this team to make this book a reality.

I appreciate especially the support of my two daughters, Emma and Bridget, and my husband, David, who is not a Mennonite but who laughs at my jokes nonetheless and never turns down a cocktail no matter how Anabaptist the recipe.

Conversion Chart

Measurements are in US fluid ounces (oz) in the book.

US fluid ounces	US customary	Metric
¼ oz	½ Tbsp / 1½ tsp	7.5 mL
⅓ oz	2 tsp	10 mL
½ oz	1 Tbsp	15 mL
¾ oz	1½ Tbsp / 4½ tsp	22 mL
1 oz (1 shot)	2 Tbsp	30 mL
1¼ oz	2½ Tbsp	37.5 mL
1½ oz	3 Tbsp	45 mL
2 oz	¼ cup	60 mL
2½ oz	5 Tbsp	75 mL
3 oz	¼ cup + 2 Tbsp	90 mL
3½ oz	¼ cup + 3 Tbsp	105 mL
4 oz	½ cup	125 mL
4½ oz	½ cup + 1 Tbsp	140 mL
5 oz	½ cup + 2 Tbsp	155 mL
5½ oz	½ cup + 3 Tbsp	170 mL
6 oz	¾ cup	185 mL
6½ oz	¾ cup + 1 Tbsp	200 mL
7 oz	¾ cup + 2 Tbsp	215 mL
7½ oz	¾ cup + 3 Tbsp	230 mL
8 oz	1 cup	250 mL
9 oz	1 cup + 2 Tbsp	280 mL

US fluid ounces	US customary	Metric
10 oz	1¼ cups	310 mL
11 oz	1¼ cups + 2 Tbsp	340 mL
12 oz	1½ cups	375 mL
16 oz	2 cups	500 mL
20 oz	2½ cups	625 mL
24 oz	3 cups	750 mL
28 oz	3½ cups	875 mL
32 oz	4 cups / 1 quart	1 L

Index

Note: Bolded text indicates recipes included in this book.

The information in this book is true and complete to the best of the author's knowledge. All recommendations are made without guarantee on the part of the author or the publisher.

Edited by Grace Yaginuma
Cover and interior design by Tree Abraham

CATALOGUING DATA AVAILABLE FROM LIBRARY AND ARCHIVES CANADA
ISBN 9781771513586 (hardcover)
ISBN 9781771513593 (electronic)

TouchWood Editions acknowledges that the land on which we live and work is within the traditional territories of the Lkwungen (Esquimalt and Songhees), Malahat, Pacheedaht, Scia'new, T'Sou-ke and W̱SÁNEĆ (Pauquachin, Tsartlip, Tsawout, Tseycum) peoples.

We acknowledge the financial support of the Government of Canada through the Canada Book Fund, and the province of British Columbia through the Book Publishing Tax Credit.

This book was produced using FSC®-certified, acid-free papers, processed chlorine-free, and printed with soya-based inks.

Printed in China

25 24 23   2 3 4 5